FINANCIAL
ACCOUNTING

Crucial Study Guides for Business Degree Courses

Titles in the series

Financial Accounting	ISBN 1 903337 00 3	Price £9.99
Business Information Systems	ISBN 1 903337 01 1	Price £9.99
Economics	ISBN 1 903337 02 X	Price £9.99
Business Law	ISBN 1 903337 03 8	Price £9.99
Organisational Behaviour	ISBN 1 903337 04 6	Price £9.99
Quantitative Methods	ISBN 1 903300 05 4	Price £9.99

To order, please contact our distributors:

Plymbridge Distributors, Estover Road, Plymouth, PL6 7PY
Tel: 01752 202301. Fax: 01752 202333. Email: orders@plymbridge.com.
www.plymbridge.com

FINANCIAL
ACCOUNTING

David Floyd

First published in 2001 by Crucial, a division of Learning Matters Ltd.

© David Floyd

British Library Cataloguing in Publication Data
A CIP record for this book is available from the British Library.

ISBN 1 903337 00 3

Crucial
58 Wonford Road
Exeter EX2 4LQ
Tel: 01392 215560
Email: info@crucial.uk.com
www.crucial.uk.com

Cover and text design by Topics – The Creative Partnership
Project Management by Deer Park Productions
Typeset by PDQ Typesetting
Printed and bound in Great Britain by Bell & Bain Ltd., Glasgow

Contents

STUDYING FINANCIAL ACCOUNTING AT
DEGREE LEVEL

Summary

Welcome to the world of higher education! You've worked to get here, and must have studied efficiently and successfully to have achieved your current qualifications. That's a good foundation on which we can build – but it is a foundation only, because you'll now find that study at degree level becomes harder. What we therefore do in this chapter is to explain how you need to develop, and the differences you will now find, as an undergraduate student.

This Chapter outlines the general principles of effective study at degree level, and how these principles apply specifically to financial accounting. You will discover how you can:

- learn efficiently from your class contact time and textbooks;

- make the best use of your learning centre and its resources (e.g. the Internet, the financial press and published accounts); and

- prepare successfully for practical exercises, coursework, presentations and examinations.

Good practice

Although studying is a personal thing, there are various 'basics' you need to know and follow. You'll have come across these at A-level/GNVQ, but will now find that they become even more important at degree level. In particular:

1. Managing your time

You've got to be realistic when calculating **when**, and **how much time**, you have available to study financial accounting. Make sure you set objectives that are achievable: if you don't do this, you'll get depressed by not achieving what you set out (unrealistically) to achieve.

2. Following instructions

Lectures, time in class, even study on the Internet provide you with valuable academic information, and they are also ways of giving you instructions about important dates, background reading, and so on. However, as an undergraduate you become even more responsible for organising your own learning. Always ensure with your tutors that you're quite clear about not only the academic information, but also the **instructions,** that they give you.

3. Arranging to study

You need to plan **where, when** and **how**. As an undergraduate, you'll now have to do even more of your work when other students are about (e.g. in halls of residence). This means that it's even more important to **choose somewhere suitable**, where you have some space and can concentrate. From your experience in school and college, you'll know these are key principles:

- study when you are not too tired;
- select the best time for studying to suit you; and
- set yourself time targets for studying – you need to take breaks to remain fresh.

Section I	**Learning from lectures, taught sessions, seminars and tutorials**

One of the first differences you'll notice in higher education is the teaching. Lectures and seminars are more commonly found, with the 'mass lecture' being a quite different experience to the normal A-level/GNVQ taught session. Your challenge is to make sure you end up with a good record of what's been said and taught.

Let's start by identifying what you **don't** need: a verbatim account of every single word uttered by your lecturer. Why not?

- The words are the lecturer's, not yours – and it is always more difficult to use and learn someone else's words rather than your own.

- It's both impossible and pointless to remember every word: there's no point trying to memorise them, since the higher education (HE) questions you will meet get you to **apply** your knowledge and understanding to **unfamiliar** situations. Although this is not a different approach from that which you've already experienced, it becomes more challenging.

- You can't write volumes while, at the same time, listening to and understanding what is being said. Students new to HE – like you! – often feel the need to copy everything down but soon discover this simply can't be done. Your tutors will expect you to summarise your thoughts so why not start here, with note-making.

What, then, is required at degree level? You will probably need – and want – to make notes of what's been explained. Notice that I'm using the phrase 'make notes' rather than 'take notes'. Note-**making** is the more demanding activity and usually expected in undergraduates, since you have to create your own record rather than simply copy down chunks of information from an acetate, the board or live off the teacher's handouts.

 Crucial tip

Remember the acronym 'POS', to remind you to:
- **Prioritise** – identify the most important points being made;
- **Organise** – use a suitable structure of headings and subheadings; and
- **Summarise** – note down the main ideas and phrases.

Lectures and taught sessions

In degree-level financial accounting sessions, the lecturer normally introduces new subject-matter, works through illustrations and problems, and explores issues arising from private study. You'll be particularly familiar with the first two from your past studies. Traditional 'one-way' lectures are still used to teach degree-level financial accounting, though when compared with many other HE subjects there's often greater emphasis on taught sessions. If you have a series of lectures, remember to **treat them as a two-way process** if possible, taking any opportunity to ask questions during or at the end of the lecture. Even if there is not this opportunity, you will still be active through summarising, organising and prioritising what is said.

Here's an extract – part of the introduction – from a taught session on depreciation of fixed assets that I recently delivered to undergraduates. The extract is accompanied by a diagram showing notes made by one of the students.

You already know how SSAP 12 defines depreciation: it is essentially how we measure the reduction in value of fixed assets over time. You are also familiar with the accruals, or matching, concept, which is the key concept underpinning the need for us to depreciate these assets.

Why fixed assets? These last for longer than one accounting period, and contribute to the firm's revenue over these periods. What we must therefore do is to allocate – i.e. charge – the cost of these assets over these accounting periods. In other words, we are spreading the cost of the fixed asset over its economic life. Thus the relevance of the accruals concept, which requires us to match expenses and revenues to the periods to which they relate.

How does depreciation arise in practice? Bear in mind the range of fixed assets existing in the real world. For example, a primary sector business such as a quarrying or mining company will need to depreciate its quarries or mines because they become depleted: we sometimes call them 'wasting assets'. We are more used to the typical fixed assets of machinery, equipment and vehicles: these may simply wear out over time, but bear in mind the increasingly common use of technology-based fixed assets, such as computers or 'high-tech' equipment, which often becomes obsolete in three or four years. As a final illustration, some assets may have a predetermined life, and need to be amortised – in other words, depreciated – over this life: leasehold property and patents are popular examples.

DEPRECIATION

Defined – see SSAP 12 note
               – basic point = reduction in FA over time
Key concept = accruals. Relevant since FA last › 1 a/c period, so must spread cost of FA across these periods.

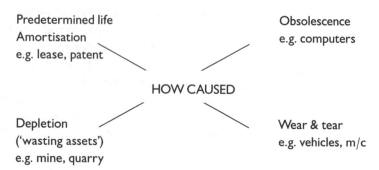

Predetermined life
Amortisation
e.g. lease, patent

Obsolescence
e.g. computers

HOW CAUSED

Depletion
('wasting assets')
e.g. mine, quarry

Wear & tear
e.g. vehicles, m/c

Let's compare the two. Notice how the student has successfully applied 'POS':

- She has **prioritised** what was said, by omitting descriptive language and through the use of key headings.

- In **organising** her notes, the student has used two different layouts: the standard 'linear' approach is followed by a non-linear one (the 'how caused' note). This gives **variety**, which will help her to remember the content when she revises.

- **Summarising** is through the use of abbreviations. This is good practice, though if you're uncomfortable with this, do remember that you can **re-write** and/or **expand** your notes afterwards. This is a particularly valuable (and often overlooked) approach, and will help **reinforce** your learning.

 Crucial tip | In financial accounting at degree level, tutors will often summarise information by using abbreviations and accounting 'jargon'. Make sure you ask for a translation if necessary!

Can we improve the above? Certainly, the content has been recorded accurately and summarised well. However, if this is to be her final record, our student has left little room for any **additional information** to be added later. In HE we expect students not only to **cross-reference** – above, our student cross-references to a definition of depreciation that she's noted elsewhere – but also to **add** extra notes, e.g. after reading textbooks. A useful tip is to **leave a margin** for these 'extras', although using a non-linear approach, such as the one shown above, usually leads to more space being left into which you can add information later.

 Crucial tip | Adding additional information is a key approach that distinguishes the good student from the ordinary one. You already know that it's insufficient simply to regurgitate the tutor's notes. To succeed at degree level, you will certainly be expected to show evidence of additional reading and further study.

Numerical work in lectures and taught sessions is a major feature of teaching financial accounting in HE. The lecturer may **demonstrate** the answer, e.g. by using an acetate or handout. What you must do here is to not only compare the **completeness** and **accuracy** of your answer, but also its **layout**. The importance of this last point is often overlooked by financial accounting undergraduates, so make sure that your use of columns and headings and the general layout of your figures matches that of your lecturer's.

 Crucial tip | At this level of study, as with A-levels and GNVQs, you're being measured against set standards rather than against other students. Consider helping each other to reach these standards, e.g. by comparing lecture notes and numerical workings, and then discussing **what** you've included/excluded/calculated, and **why**. This develops your analytical skills, which are so important in higher education.

Seminars and tutorials
These are key elements in HE. You are likely to be actively involved in seminars and tutorials, through being given problems, case studies, final

accounts, etc. to study, as well as relevant chapters of your textbook(s) to read. You will find that these activities are not only necessary at degree level, but are also well worth doing.

How do good HE students make the best use of seminars and tutorials? Although you'll get some benefit from copying down the answers and comments made by others during tutorials, workshops or seminars, there are four clear benefits to you of doing advance preparation:

- it gives you a **fuller coverage** of the content;
- you can now efficiently and easily **compare others' thoughts with your own**;
- you will have gone through the thought processes that are **vital preparation** for your HE exam and other assessment; and
- it gives you the chance to **identify difficult or confusing content**.

 Crucial tip — Make good use of your tutorials: this time is valuable to you, and may well be limited because of student numbers and/or your tutor's other commitments. To do so, don't bring along loads of information that your tutor hasn't seen before and is expected to read during the tutorial: e-mail or otherwise send it in advance, to make best use of this limited time.

Section 2 — Learning from textbooks

Some of the more popular textbooks recommended for first-year accounting students are:

Britton, A. and Waterston, C. (1999) *Financial Accounting*, 2nd edn. Longman.

Dodge, Roy (1997) *Foundations of Business Accounting*, 2nd edn. International Thomson Business Press.

Glautier, M.W. E. and Underdown, B. (1997) *Accounting Theory and Practice*, 6th edn. Financial Times Pitman Publishing.

Johnson, H. and Whitram, A., revised Crawford, M. (1996) *A Practical Foundation in Accounting*, 5th edn. International Thomson Business Press.

Thomas, A. (1996) *An Introduction to Financial Accounting*, 2nd edn. McGraw-Hill.

Wood, F. and Sangster, A. (1999) *Business Accounting 1*, 8th edn. Financial Times Pitman Publishing.

 Crucial tip — It's important to get the most up-to-date version of your book, since it will include more of the recent changes to financial accounting (e.g. on FRSs). Check with your booksellers whether these are the most recent editions.

Getting value from your book

Which textbook(s) should you buy? Obviously **follow your lecturer's advice**, since they will know the extent to which the textbook matches the content of your module/unit. However, unlike many A-level and GNVQ texts, these general textbooks have not been written exclusively for your module/unit so it will be helpful for you to obtain more than one of them if possible. Financial accounting books can be expensive, and one way of coping with this cost is to arrange with friends to buy different books and to share these resources.

Since the study of degree-level financial accounting involves a lot of worked numerical exercises, a key question for you to ask is: **does the book have clear, worked answers?** In practice, you may find that you now have less access to your tutor than you had in school and college, so – other things being equal – it is better to obtain a book that **shows you how the answer is obtained**, rather than one that simply includes the answer without providing workings.

 Crucial tip

If you have a book that only provides limited explanation of how an answer is obtained, don't forget the value of (a) tutorial and workshop time spent with your lecturer, and (b) sharing resources with friends.

Here are two questions you need to answer:

- Should you **personalise your book**? If you want or need to resell it, the temptation is to keep the book in as near-new a condition as possible – but that really defeats the object of buying it in the first place! Books are there to be read, and that means they must suffer some 'wear and tear' damage. It's pointless at this level of study to get a book and then not make the best use of it. Why not consider using a highlighter pen, or otherwise marking important workings or sections (remember the value of **prioritising** information)? You may find that this 'personalising' not only identifies these key areas and helps you access them quickly and easily, but also helps you **remember** and **apply** the information.

- Should you **copy information**? Again, this is a personal decision. Some A-level and GNVQ students value the act of copying out huge chunks of information, arguing that it helps them 'learn' the information. Certainly, if you adapt the information to **your own needs**, e.g. by changing the wording or the structure to something more meaningful to you as an undergraduate student, there will still be a benefit from this activity at degree level. However you choose to do it, it is important to **link the book's content to your notes**. For example, leaving a margin in your notes – as suggested earlier – will allow you to integrate textbook information easily and efficiently. Also, remember that you are now being increasingly assessed on your ability to **do** things with the information you know: few marks are available in HE financial accounting for memorising and copying out basic information.

Crucial tip

In degree-level financial accounting, as with any HE subject, you will need to **acknowledge the source** of any external information you choose to include in your assignments or other work.

Doing accounts questions from books

There is a major benefit to be gained from doing these questions and studying/comparing your answers with those of the book and of your friends, because you gain an insight into **how** the answer is constructed. Also, 'the more the merrier': the more questions you tackle on any one topic, the more familiar you'll become with the possible variations – and there is only a finite number of these – that you may meet in your HE examination.

Crucial tip

You should already be in the habit of **showing all your workings**. This remains important in higher education, with marks being awarded for both **method** – knowing how you do or calculate something – and **accuracy** (getting it right). If you make an error and therefore lose the 'accuracy' marks, you can still gain the 'method' marks for showing your examiner that you know the correct approach to use.

Other important published sources

Because you are now an undergraduate student it is particularly important to get into the habit of (occasionally, at least!) reading the financial section of a 'broadsheet' newspaper such as *The Times, Guardian* or *Telegraph*. Also, do try to keep up to date by checking the articles in the major accounting journals. This approach is another way to get your tutor to distinguish and 'label' you as a good, rather than an average, student.

Relevant publications include:

- *Accountancy* – Institute of Chartered Accountants in England and Wales;
- *Certified Accountant* – Association of Chartered Certified Accountants;
- *Management Accounting* – Chartered Institute of Management Accountants;
- *Chartered Secretary* – Institute of Chartered Secretaries and Administrators.

Other relevant publications include *Accountancy Age, The Economist* and *Management Today.*

Crucial tip

A word of warning, however: these publications will include information which does not relate exclusively to your module/unit, or which may cover the topic you are studying in more depth than you really require.

Tackling your text

You often find in HE that your tutor has produced what seems like a never-ending reading list to work through.

 Crucial tip Here's a particularly valuable tip: make sure you get clear guidance from your tutors regarding which books are particularly useful for which topics, to help you prioritise your reading and study time.

Reading efficiently is very important at degree level, helping to distinguish the better students from others — it's not all about taking out the greatest number of books from your Learning Centre! Whenever about to undertake some reading, ask yourself the question: **why am I reading?** There are three typical reasons:

- to obtain an **overall picture** of a topic;
- to get **full information** about an idea or concept; and
- to **answer a specific question**.

One popular approach that works well at HE level, helping you to identify the relevance or importance of the accounting texts you are reading, is **SQ3R**. This was originally developed by Francis Robinson, and stands for:

SURVEY

Identify the 'general drift' from the text, looking for clues about what it contains. At this stage, you are not trying to learn the content. Key **questions** you need to ask and answer at this stage are:

- Do I want/need to read this? (Your accounting tutor will help to answer this question.)
- (If 'yes':) What information am I going to find here? (Again, your tutor will help.)
- What quality of information is here (up-to-date, detailed, structured logically)?

Key **clues** to help you at this stage include checking the date of publication, the contents list and index, headings and subheading used, the use of diagrams or other summaries of information, and chapter introductions and conclusions.

To survey a book, check:	To survey a chapter, check:
Title page/preface	Headings and subheadings
Contents list/index	First and final paragraphs

QUESTION

You should identify a number of questions that you want answering: these questions will provide the **focus** for your research. Examples of commonly asked questions include:

- What financial accounting information is new to me here?
- How does this relate to what I already know about financial accounting?
- Is this fact or the author's opinion?
- Is this up to date?
- Why has the author structured the topic in this way?

READ

Note that this is the third step, not the first! You read fully through the text, but keep in mind the questions you want answering. Check for key phrases and accounting terms – often identified in the text by italics, underlining or other methods of emphasising – but don't make notes at this stage (this slows you down and acts as a distraction). A lot of HE students find it useful to **reread** the information.

RECALL

This stage tests that you've **remembered** and **understood** the financial accounting information you've read. At the end of an appropriate section – a paragraph if the ideas are complex, a worked set of accounts, or a longer section if more straightforward – take a break from the text and recall what you have read by **making notes** (this also helps build up your concentration).

REVIEW

Here you are checking the **accuracy** of your recall. You can assess this by asking:

- Have I answered my questions?
- Can I recall all key points?
- Is my recall accurate and thorough?

Section 3:	Using libraries and related resources

Your HE institution will no doubt have its own website, where you'll find valuable information concerning your library/resource centre. In all probability, you'll be able to **search** for, and to **order** or **reserve**, library books using an electronic database. Your library is also likely to subscribe to the publications of the various accountancy bodies, as well as having newspapers with financial pages and 'hard copy' editions of PLCs' published accounts for you to study.

How do HE students use **ICT** – information and communications technology – effectively when studying financial accounting? Essentially, through **accessing** information and **using** it as a tool for **communicating**. The Internet is, of course, increasingly important as an information source. Important accounting body web addresses are:

- http://www.cima.org.uk/
  The Chartered Institute of Management Accountants

- http://www.icaew.co.uk/
  The Institute of Chartered Accountants in England & Wales

- http://www.acca.org.uk/
  The Association of Chartered Certified Accountants

- http://www.cipfa.org.uk/
  The Chartered Institute of Public Finance & Accountancy

- http://www.icsa.org.uk/
  The Institute of Chartered Secretaries & Administrators

Financial information can also be obtained from publishers' websites. Examples include:

- http://www.ft.com/   *The Financial Times*
- http://www.the-times.co.uk/   *The Times*
- http://www.guardian.co.uk/   *The Guardian*
- http://www.independent.co.uk/   *The Independent*
- http://www.economist.com/   *The Economist*

Other relevant sites include those of PLCs, through which you can often obtain copies of their published accounts. Examples include:

- http://www.sainsburys.co.uk/   Sainsbury's
- http://www.tesco.co.uk/   Tesco's

 Crucial tip

Published accounts are a valuable source of real-life financial accounting information, but make sure you are not intimidated at first by their complexity and detail. You will gradually become more knowledgeable about the terms, concepts, notes and layout of these accounts.

The information available from your library and these other sources tends to be quite reliable: sites with **.org**, **.gov** and **.com** also normally contain reliable information. Some other websites that are apparently relevant to financial accounting students may, however, contain information that is either inaccurate, incomplete or out of date. There are four **quality indicators** you can use to assess web-based information:

- What is its **authority?** Is there full information about the ownership of the page, e.g. name, postal address, e-mail, phone number?

- Is it **accurate?** Is the information verifiable and well written (spelling, punctuation and grammar), and are there hyperlinks to other related pages?

- Is it **current?** What is the date of the document?

- Is it **biased?** What balance is there between the 'selling' of services and the objectivity of the information?

We can add a fifth one for undergraduate financial accounting students: because accounting principles vary between the UK and the USA, does the site contain **UK-specific** information?

An important trend in higher education is where tutors place information and tasks onto their institution's intranet site. Your module/unit guides probably contain web addresses and/or have structured activities that you can study using this site.

 Crucial tip Learning centre (library) staff are a valuable resource to you by being able to provide advice about the institution's financial accounting-specific resources, particularly those that are electronic-based.

Although we often regard working with computers as a two-way process, the inevitable system crash or query that the computer can't answer will make it feel very much a one-way activity. These situations commonly occur in degree-level study, since you will often be working outside the traditional classroom environment.

- In such situations, you should note any areas of difficulty for future 'in person' tutorials and workshops.

- You can also use ICT to overcome some of the problems created when using it in the first place. Your tutor will have an e-mail address: since tutors are busy people, sending an e-mail will be an important way for you to stay in touch.

Section 4: Preparing for presentations

Another key trend in higher education is to make students give a lot of presentations, and – while not as widely found as in other subjects – this is no exception for financial accounting. One popular example is when you are asked to produce some form of financial plan which must be presented to a panel of (real or fictional) experts.

We use presentations at degree level to assess your ability to **collect**, **analyse**, **organise** and **summarise** information, and the quality of your **explanation**. You will have undertaken a number of presentations already, and may be used to presenting information both orally and in writing. The better presentations at HE level are assessed on the same main criteria:

- well organised and suitably summarised information;
- outlined in clear statements by the presenters;
- who link well together;
- who take into account the audience.

There is an increasing expectation in higher education that presentations should be 'professional'. Your learning centre's computer network will almost certainly contain a package such as Microsoft's **PowerPoint**. This presentation software is very useful: using it to produce slides, either generated via a computer presentation or copied onto acetate, gets you to plan **what to say** as well as **the order** in which you are going to say it. The use of such packages also forces you to think about **structure** and the **key points** you need to summarise.

 Crucial tip

Using PowerPoint for presentations is a valuable 'insurance' that the basics of your presentation (layout, appearance, etc.) will be good. However, don't overlook the fact that the better students realise that this technology won't solve the problem of **tailoring the subject-matter to the audience**. Presentations offering thought-out opinion, backed up with suitable evidence, will achieve the best results.

Although some students prepare a full script of what they will say, I wouldn't recommend this approach because such presentations are often limited to reading exclusively from the script. This results in a very 'dry' and boring presentation. You will need back-up notes, though, and PowerPoint or similar presentation packages allow you to create 'notes pages' on which you can produce sufficiently detailed presenter notes that act as an effective prompt.

We can use the acronym 'LOST SIR' to identify the main general issues when making a presentation in financial accounting:

- **Look** at the audience.
- **Organise** your slides and notes.
- **Speak** slowly and clearly.
- **Tone** of your voice needs varying.
- **Seeing** your projected information is important for the audience!
- **Impact** at the start, e.g. by a diagram or cartoon if appropriate, attracts attention.
- **Rehearse** your timing, comments and links in advance.

Crucial tip

What, then, are the key questions that need answering to plan a good undergraduate presentation in financial accounting? They are:

- What objectives do I have?
- Who is my audience?
- Do they know the financial accounting terms and language I'm proposing to use?
- Are my figures accurate, legible and laid out correctly?

Section 5: Coping with coursework and examinations

Practical exercises and coursework feature strongly in HE financial accounting modules. They will be word-based, number-based, or a combination of the two. At degree level, traditional time-constrained exams contain a similar mix of questions, and remain an extremely popular method of assessing your ability to construct and explain the nature of financial accounts.

The key skills at this level being assessed are your ability to:

- **organise yourself** through managing your own time and resources, and by setting personal objectives;

- **work effectively**, both on your own and with others;

- **use information and communications technology (ICT)** in order to retrieve, manipulate and send numerical and other data relevant to financial accounting;

- **process numerical information** such as final accounts;

- **analyse and interpret the results** of your numerical work;

- **draw appropriate conclusions** in solving problems shown by the financial accounts; and

- **communicate clearly** these results and any key financial accounting terms and ideas, both through writing and by making presentations.

Word-based coursework and examination questions

For degree-level work, you will normally be required to show your understanding by describing, explaining and analysing some aspect of financial accounting. The question may contain these or similar **action verbs** that tell you what is expected: examples, in typical order of difficulty, are 'State…', 'Describe…', 'Analyse…' and 'Evaluate…'. You may be familiar with this approach already, for example in A-level exams. If not, here are the key meanings of these terms:

- **State** requires you to list, name or otherwise simply write down basic information.

- **Describe** means that you must put the information you know into your own words.

- **Analyse** requires you to take an argument or idea apart, breaking it down into its key elements.

- **Evaluate** is the most difficult to achieve, since you must analyse an idea or concept and then make a clear judgement of its worth or relevance.

In all cases, it pays to **plan your structure** so the assessor can follow your points. You may receive credit for drawing a **valid** conclusion: not one that merely repeats the arguments you have already outlined, but one where you evaluate all the evidence presented and then make relevant statements concerning this evidence.

 Crucial tip   You receive no credit for repetition, so make your points clearly and precisely.

Here is a short-answer question, together with an extract from a student's answer.

> **Question.** Delivery vehicles owned by Lee Ltd are presently depreciated using the reducing balance method. The company secretary has asked the Chief Accountant to consider switching to using the straight-line method. Evaluate whether the company should change its method of calculating depreciation.

> **Answer.** When using the reducing balance method of depreciation, a fixed percentage is applied to the written-down value of the fixed asset each year. As a result of using this 'accelerated method' of depreciation, more depreciation is charged in the asset's early years than in later years, and is therefore a suitable method when fixed assets such as vehicles lose much of their value at or near the start of their lives. As the vehicle ages, its lower depreciation cost is typically offset by higher maintenance costs, thereby tending to even out the total cost associated with this asset. Although this method may therefore be appropriate for delivery vehicles, it can be difficult to establish a suitable percentage rate to use. Also, should the company decide to vary this rate, there are implications for disclosure: SSAP 12 states that a change from one method to another is allowable only if the new method will give a fairer presentation of a company's financial position.
> Will the straight-line method give a fairer presentation in this situation? It uses a formula for its calculation…

The first two sentences in the answer illustrate factual statements and description. The rest of the answer supports this by good analysis and an evaluation of the one method contained in this extract.

Number-based coursework and exam questions

At any level of study in financial accounting, you need to be able to handle numbers. Although the emphasis at degree level is on **applying** your knowledge and **evaluating** the results, the quality of your evaluation largely depends on the accuracy of your calculations. You already know that you will receive some marks for accurate calculations, so be prepared to use a calculator. At HE level it is more important than ever to show your workings: this makes a big difference when your answers are assessed.

Crucial tip
Don't automatically rely on the result shown by your calculator: **estimate** your answer first. This acts as a logical check to ensure that you haven't pressed a wrong button. Remember: does the answer **look** right?

Revising for examinations

In HE you will be left more and more to organise your own learning and study time. This includes checking exam details, so make sure you know **where** the exam is and **how long** it is. You are probably well aware of the 'basics' of revision, such as the need to revise well in advance, and the value of staggering your revision to avoid over-long sessions. For financial accounting undergraduate exams in particular, a good tip is to study all the past papers you can get hold of – check their availability with your tutors and library staff. This gives you a 'feel' for the type of questions, and the time pressure involved (this is often a major problem for financial accounting students).

Crucial tip
Your HE exams, unlike A-levels, are not nationally set and marked. Pay close attention to your tutor's remarks – your tutor quite probably set the paper!

What exactly is 'revision'? Much of your revising to date will have involved learning and memorising a lot of information, and you'll have devised approaches to this which probably work well for you. This activity is still relevant to a certain extent, both in HE and for our particular subject, but it certainly doesn't tell the full story. Furthermore, at this level you can't get away with last-minute revision because you won't be assessed on what you've managed to cram into your short-term memory! What a well-organised and efficient undergraduate should do on a regular basis is to **revisit** work:

- by re-reading it, you identify weaknesses in your knowledge, and can work on these rather than face a last-minute panic and loss of confidence;

- by adding margin notes or further worked examples to your work, you can draw things together as well as extend your knowledge; and

- by manipulating the information you're studying, you become more effective in analysing and evaluating it.

This type of revision depends upon your ability to **manage your time efficiently**. It pays dividends, especially in financial accounting since you are in some ways learning a 'skill' (constructing an account, balancing it, following a set layout, etc.). And, like any skill, the more you do it the better you become at it!

Taking examinations

Here are some 'sensible activity' tips for a degree-level examination in financial accounting:

- **Read** the paper extremely carefully. If there is a choice, study the alternatives – don't rush in, since degree-level financial accounting questions can at first glance appear to be more difficult than they really are.

- Allocate your **time** carefully, and don't spend too long on any one question. Many students spend too much time on trying to get a balance sheet to balance – and you may have only one error causing this imbalance, which means you've earned nearly all available marks! You face the 'opportunity cost' of losing what may be relatively easy marks in a question you now have no time to answer.

- Remember that you get **nothing for 'waffle'** in HE. Time spent repeating yourself is better spent on tackling number-based questions, which are often more time-consuming at this level.

- We expect your words and numbers to be **legible**, and that you will follow **orthodox financial accounting layout**. It is usually better to cross a wrong figure out and insert the correct figure above or below it, rather than to try altering the original figure.

- And, yet again, a reminder to show those workings.

 Crucial tip — Visit your exam room in advance to get familiar with its appearance and likely layout. This helps you cope with nerves 'on the day'.

CHAPTER 1

INFORMATION

Chapter summary

Financial accounting is concerned with obtaining, recording and using financial information to make decisions. This Chapter sets the scene for the rest of the book through explaining how financial accounting relates to other branches of accounting, and by describing the main users of financial information in our economy.

Studying this Chapter will help you to:

- distinguish between financial accounting, management accounting, auditing and taxation;

- describe the main profit-making forms of ownership in the private sector of the UK economy; and

- name the main internal and external users of financial information, and explain their main interest.

Assessment targets

Target 1: using business terms appropriately

Throughout your assessments, you will be required to describe and use business terms appropriately. Exercise 1 at the end of the Chapter tests you on this.

Target 2: describing the users of financial information

In your assessment, you may be asked to show your understanding of the different groups that are interested in financial information. Exercise 2 assesses your ability to do this.

Target 3: explaining the relationship between the users of, and nature of, financial information

You will be expected not only to know and describe the various groups involved with financial information: you will also have to explain their specific interest(s) in this information. Exercise 3 at the end of the Chapter tests this knowledge.

Crucial concepts

These are the key terms and concepts you will meet in this Chapter:

Financial adaptability	Liquidity
Financial performance	PLC
Financial position	Profitability
Limited company	Stewardship
Limited liability	Unlimited liability

Relevant links

Chapters 4–6 apply your knowledge of the types of business organisation to constructing 'final accounts'. Chapter 8 develops the role of financial information by introducing you to accounting ratios and the analysis of financial performance.

What are you studying?

In this section we look at a definition of financial accounting and learn what it means. The definition gets us thinking about why an organisation's managers **need** financial information, and how they **use** it.

How will you be assessed on this?

You don't need to memorise a definition of financial accounting since you won't be tested on your ability just to recall basic information. What you will be tested on is your understanding of what financial accounting is, and how it fits into the overall decision-making framework of business. This section therefore provides you with the knowledge you need when answering questions to do with the role of financial accounting.

You will come across various definitions of financial accounting in your studies. It is often defined along these lines:

> Recording, summarising and analysing an organisation's transactions and activities in order to provide useful information for its owners, managers and other stakeholders.

How do we explain this in your book? You'll study the **recording** of transactions and activities in Chapters 2 and 3. Chapters 4, 5 and 6 show how the **financial statements** of the main organisations in our economy are constructed, and illustrate how they differ.

In addition to historical information showing the results of **past activities**, detailed information will be needed so that management can carry out the functions of:

- **planning** – through the planning process, managers can identify what must be done in order to help achieve the aims of the firm (examples include **budgeting**);

- **controlling** – the activities that take place must be managed properly, monitored closely and controlled efficiently;

- **making decisions** – management must focus on how, given a number of alternatives, to select the the best course of action so the firm can meet its objectives and targets.

Management is particularly interested in the following:

- How much **profit** has the firm made in a given time period – or, for a non-profit-making organisation, how does its income compare with its expenditure?

- What does it **own**, and what does it **owe** to others?

- How likely is it to **survive** in today's competitive world?

Crucial tip   Study how the three points above link with:
(a) the 3 financial statements on page 25, and
(b) the external and internal users of this information (figure 1.2).

Financial accounting is one of the main branches of accounting. Managers take the information recorded in accounts – its **book-keeping** role – and interpret and present this information.

You will meet some or all of the other main branches of accounting during your studies. These are:

1. **Management accounting**

   Unlike financial accounting, management accounting collects and analyses financial information for **internal** purposes. We have already seen that managers seek to plan, control and make decisions: management accounting provides **costing**, **budgeting** and other information to help managers.

	Financial accounting:	**Management accounting:**
is prepared for:	*external reporting;*	*internal use;*
is presented:	*in a way dictated by external bodies/legal requirements;*	*in a way designed by the firm's management;*
consists of:	*financial information;*	*financial and non-financial information;*
is concerned with:	*past data;*	*past data and future data.*

2. **Auditing**

   Once information has been collected and accounts have been prepared, **external auditors** may be employed to check the fairness and accuracy of these accounts. (For some business organisations, such as limited companies, this is a legal requirement.) The role of these external auditors is to protect the interests of the company's shareholders. **Internal auditors** are also found: unlike external auditors, they are employees of the company who will check the company's various book-keeping and accounting procedures.

3. **Taxation**

   Accountants may choose to specialise in taxation, seeking to reduce their clients' tax bills – **tax avoidance** rather than **tax evasion**. Clients include sole traders, partners and limited company organisations.

Crucial concept

Tax **avoidance** is the (legal) attempt to reduce a client's tax bill to its absolute minimum: tax **evasion** is the illegal non-declaration of taxable income.

Quick check

1. Name and describe three functions of management.
2. Distinguish between:
    (a) book-keeping and financial accounting;
    (b) financial accounting and management accounting.

Section 2 — Types of private sector organisation

What are you studying?

This section outlines the nature of, and difference between, the main types of business ownership found in the private (profit-making) sector of our economy. The key differences are reflected in these organisations' financial statements, which we study in Chapters 4–6.

How will you be assessed on this?

Although you are not likely to have to explain in depth the nature of these forms of private sector ownership, there are certain key concepts to do with each of them that influence how each form undertakes its accounting. Your knowledge of these concepts will be tested mainly in questions on final accounts (financial statements).

Figure 1.1 summarises the main organisations in the UK economy. At this stage of your study of financial accounting, you'll be concentrating on the main organisations found in the private sector.

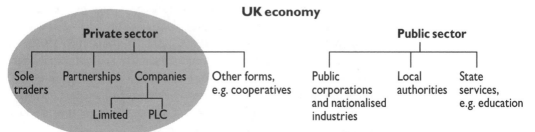

Figure 1.1 The main types of organisation in the UK economy

We know that **private sector** firms are owned by individuals, rather than by the state, and that these owners – **entrepreneurs** – seek to make **profit** by producing and selling their goods and services. The firm's ability to **survive** is another important objective for us to consider when constructing the accounts.

Crucial tip

A firm can survive in the short term even if making losses: its liquidity (see page 26) is the key measure of its ability to survive.

Sole traders and partnerships

A typical example of a sole trader is the traditional 'corner shop'. Partnerships are again traditionally associated with the professions, such as accountants and lawyers.

Crucial tip   Many people can be employed by a sole trader organisation: the term 'sole' refers to the fact that there is a **single owner**.

Sole traders and partnerships are examples of **unincorporated businesses**. The key features of unincorporated businesses you need to know are that:

1. These firm have no separate legal existence from their owner(s). The firms cannot enter into contracts in their own name, and the owners are responsible for business debts.

2. There is **unlimited liability** for these business debts.

Crucial concept   **Unlimited liability** means that the owners of a business have to use their personal wealth to meet any business debts that cannot be paid from their firm's resources.

The main difference in accounting terms is how **profit** is dealt with. With a sole trader, there is no problem – one person, one profit. With a partnership, however, this single profit must be **appropriated** – shared out – between (at least) two partners. We will study this in depth in Chapter 4. Another feature affecting the accounts is that the death or retirement of an existing partner, or the introduction of a new partner, means that the existing partnership ends. This also affects the partnership accounts (see page 103).

Limited companies

Unlike sole traders and partnerships, limited companies have a **separate legal existence** from that of their owners (shareholders): the company can take, and defend, legal actions in its own name. Its shareholders also have the benefit of **limited liability**.

Crucial concept   **Limited liability** means that owners of a company can only lose the amount they have invested (or have agreed to invest) in the company.

Crucial tip   Limited liability is fundamental to capitalism: people are willing to take a risk investing when they know there is a **limit** to this risk.

A simple change of shareholder – remember, they are the owners – does not cause major changes as far as the accounts are concerned, because of

continuity as a result of the separate legal existence of the company.

With companies there tends to be a **separation of ownership and control**. Unlike sole traders and partnerships, where the owners normally run the business themselves, the shareholders of a limited company elect **directors** (at the AGM – annual general meeting) who then delegate by appointing managers to run the company on a day-to-day basis.

 Crucial tip You will meet examples of the separation of ownership from control when studying the directors' and chairman's reports.

The main differences in the accounts of limited companies arise from **Companies Acts** legislation controlling their activities. For example:

- their annual accounts have to be filed with the Registrar of Companies, and are therefore available for public inspection;

- they must disclose a minimum amount of information (see Chapter 6).

Crucial concept The two classes of company are **private**, with the word 'limited' or 'ltd' at the end of their name, and **public**, with 'public limited company' or 'plc' at the end of their name. As their name suggests, PLCs can invite the public to invest in their shares

 Quick check
1. Give at least two examples from your own experience of:
   (a) sole traders   (b) partnerships
   (c) private limited   (d) public limited
       companies ('ltd')   companies.
2. Explain the difference between unlimited liability and limited liability.

Section 3 | The users of financial information

What are you studying?

The whole point of preparing accounts – and in particular the 'final accounts' – is so that people can make judgements about the financial position and performance of the firm in question. There are a number of different users of this financial information: some of them are internal to the firm, though most are external to it.

How will you be assessed on this?

You may be given an essay-type question that asks you about the **financial stewardship** of a firm, how important this is to the various user groups, and what these groups are particularly interested in. You have to show that you are aware of the differing areas of interest represented by these user groups.

Figure 1.2 provides a summary of the main users of financial information.

Crucial tip   These users are often nowadays described as **stakeholders**.

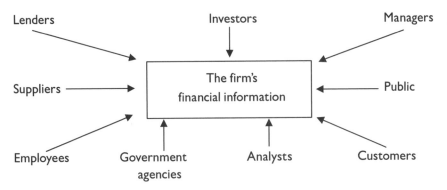

Figure 1.2 Users (stakeholders) of accounting information

Crucial tip   It is easy to remember the list by the initials: start at the top left to read (clockwise) 'LIMP CAGES'.

We can see that some of these users of financial information — managers, employees and in some cases such as sole traders or partners the investors (owners) — are **internal** to the business, whereas the rest are **external**.

How does Figure 1.2 link with the three main **financial statements** that you will be studying?

- The **profit and loss account**. This provides information on the **financial performance** of a business in terms of its **income** and **expenditure**. External users are interested in the firm's profit level and its **profitability**:

  - investors want to know the likely return on their investment;
  - government agencies are interested in individual firms' profit levels (for taxation purposes) and the country's overall economic performance (national statistics);
  - analysts in the financial press report on, and the public (who are often potential investors) read about, a PLC's profits and profitability;
  - internally, management will be judged partly on profits, and the job security of employees also depends partly on profit levels.

Crucial concept   **Profit** is a statement of what the firm has 'made': it is the difference between the firm's income and its expenditure. **Profitability** is a better measure of success and efficiency because it compares the amount of profit made with the resources used in making that profit.

Crucial tip | It's vital that you use the terms 'profit' and 'profitability' appropriately, especially when you are describing and analysing an organisation's financial performance.

- The **balance sheet**. This summarises the **financial position** of a business at a particular point in time, i.e. what it owns as **assets** and what it owes in the form of **liabilities**:

  - suppliers and other lenders/investors will evaluate the nature, quality and age of the firm's assets, e.g. to ensure any credit given or loans made have suitable 'security';
  - customers, investors and financial analysts – and, internally, managers and employees – will all be interested in the state of the firm's financial health as shown by the balance sheet.

- The **cash flow statement**. This provides information on the firm's cash movements.

  - owners, other investors and suppliers are particularly interested in the organisation's **liquidity**, wanting to check the likelihood that they will be able to get their money back if the organisation ceases to operate;
  - internally, managers and employees also wish to assess liquidity because it is a good measure of the survival prospects of the firm: poor cash flow often leads to business closure.

Crucial concept | A firm's **liquidity** is a measure of its ability to meet its debts as these debts become due for payment.

Crucial tip | A firm's liquidity is a more important guide than its profitability when assessing its chances of survival in the marketplace.

All users of financial statements need information on financial position, performance and adaptability.

Key term:	POSITION	PERFORMANCE	ADAPTABILITY
Key statement:	*Balance sheet*	*Profit and loss account*	*(All three financial*
	Cash flow statement	*Cash flow statement*	*statements)*

Crucial tip | These key terms are used in the Accounting Standards Board's *Statement of Principles* (see Chapter 6).

Crucial concept | **Financial adaptability** refers to how well an organisation can adapt to key changes in the economic environment in which it operates.

Financial statements also illustrate the results of the managers' **steward-ship** of the business.

Crucial concept | The **stewardship** of a business refers to how efficient managers are in using the resources they have been given by the owners.

Quick check
1. Name **two** internal, and **two** external, users of financial statements.
2. Explain the difference between profit and profitability.

Crucial examples

1. Explain each of these terms:

Financial adaptability	Liquidity
Financial performance	Profitability
Financial position	PLC
Limited company	Stewardship
Limited liability	Unlimited liability

2. Complete this table to show how external users make use of financial statements to assess the stewardship of management.

Organisation	Example of external users	Example of use
PLC	Shareholders	?
Partnership	?	?
Local authority	?	?
Local sports club	?	?

3. Select **one** of these external users of financial information. Explain how this group uses financial information to make financial decisions.

Answers

1. Check your answers against the **Crucial concepts** in the Chapter.
2. Make sure you have selected **external** users: exclude managers and employees. (These are examples only: you may have selected different users and/or different illustrations of use.)

Organisation	Example of external users	Example of use
Limited company	Shareholders	To evaluate their likely/actual return on the shares invested in the company.
Partnership	Government	To assess the amount of tax payable by each of the partners.
Local authority	Council tax payers	To decide whether the council is providing 'value-for-money' services.
Local sports club	Members	To discover the extent to which the club's officials are helping it meet its objectives (e.g. 'to break even financially').

3. User selected: shareholders. This group uses financial information to measure the efficiency of the company, specifically in terms of its profitability. The shareholders will be interested in the financial stability and profitability of the company, and how these influence the share prices and the level of dividends.

Crucial reading and research

Reading

These books provide more information on the background to financial statements and their users.

Dodge, R. (1997) *Foundations of Business Accounting,* 2nd edn. International Thomson Business Press. ISBN 1 86512 153 7. See Chapter 1, 'The accounting environment', users (pp. 2–3); forms of business ownership (pp. 3–9); information needs of users (pp. 11–12).

Dyson, J. R. (1994) *Accounting for Non-Accounting Students*, 3rd edn. Pitman Publishing (ISBN 0 273 50435 X). See Chapter 1, 'The accounting world', nature and purpose of accounting (pp. 4–7).

Research

In December 1999 the Accounting Standards Board (ASB) published its *Statement of Principles for Financial Reporting*. We return to this statement in Chapter 6, but here are some valuable areas for research.

1. Explore further the nature of limited companies, in particular by getting hold of a number of published accounts: you can either contact the companies directly, or you can often download the accounts from the web, or you can use your institution's learning centre resources (they will almost certainly have recent annual reports on file).

2. Once you have this information, does the annual report in your view provide information that is both **clear** and **consistent**?

3. Examine the detail of the ASB's *Statement*: in particular, what does it say about
   (a) the 'reporting entity'? (Chapter 2)
   (b) the presentation of financial information? (Chapter 7).

CHAPTER 2

DOUBLE-ENTRY
BASICS

Chapter summary

This Chapter provides the background on how 'ledger accounts' are constructed. These accounts act as records of the firm's financial transactions, and enable the accounts staff and management of the firm to assess its financial position and prospects.

Studying this Chapter will help you to:

- understand and use appropriately the various names and terms that you will meet when studying and interpreting the accounts of a firm;

- describe the approach used, and use this approach, in recording and balancing individual accounts;

- distinguish between capital and revenue expenditure, and explain why it is important to make this distinction;

- group the different types of accounts under suitable headings and into their appropriate ledgers; and

- explain how the accruals concept operates, and apply it to the accounts of a firm.

Assessment targets

Target I: carrying out basic double-entry In your assessment, you may be given a series of transactions and be asked to make book-keeping entries from them. Exercise I at the end of the Chapter assesses your ability to do this.

Target 2: explaining the account entries
You may have to describe and use account entries and balances. Exercise 2 at the end of the Chaptertests you on this.

Target 3: distinguishing between revenue and capital expenditure
You have to know these two types of expenditure. Exercise 3 at the end of the Chapter tests your ability to distinguish between them.

Target 4: using accounting terms appropriately
Throughout your assessments, you will have to use accounting terms appropriately. Exercise 4 at the end of the Chapter assesses whether you can define these terms with ease.

Crucial concepts

These are the key terms and concepts you will meet in this Chapter:

Account	Expense
Accrual	Final accounts
Accruals concept	Income (revenue)
Asset	Ledger
Balance	Liability
Book of original entry	Matching concept
Capital expenditure	Prepayment
Creditor	Revenue expenditure
Debit and credit	Source document
Debtor	Transaction

Relevant links

In Chapter 3 we use your knowledge of account balances in showing you how basic final accounts are constructed. Chapters 4–6 show how the double-entry principles outlined here translate into the structure and nature of a firm's final accounts.

Section 1 — An account

What are you studying?

In this section we outline the nature, purpose and layout of typical 'ledger accounts'. These accounts form the basis of financial accounting.

How will you be assessed on this?

To understand financial accounting, we need to be familiar with what an account is, and what it seeks to do. If your exam or coursework includes a descriptive question on accounts, you will be asked to explain what you will learn from this and related sections. While you may not be assessed directly or in depth on this content, you will certainly draw upon this knowledge when analysing financial information (which is usually given in the form of account balances).

What images come to mind when the word 'accountant' is mentioned? The traditional stereotype is of someone who has a less than exciting life, and who pays great attention to detail and to records: above all, perhaps, someone who is involved with money.

There is at least some truth in this image. Accountants are concerned primarily with money (or, more correctly, with **value**), for example in recording its movement. Money has been called 'the lifeblood of any business', and the business's **accounts** will show how it handles and uses money or value.

Accounts are used to **record the financial transactions of a business.** They provide a record of the firm's expenses, its income, what it owns and what it owes. As business transactions take place, the firm's accounts staff use the accounts to record the results of these transactions.

Crucial concept

An **account** records the movement in value of the item/person named at its head, e.g. the Purchases a/c (account) records the movement in value of purchases; the Vehicles a/c records the changes in value of the firm's vehicles.

Another, related, way of describing an account is to think of it as a **history** of some aspect of the firm's business. Here is an example of a customer's account: its content shows the firm's dealings with, and relationship to, this customer.

Crucial tip

Relate the account name to each transaction shown in the account, working through these transactions in date order.

AL Ltd Account

		£				£
January 1	Balance	400				
			January 5	Bank		380
				Discount		20
January 12	Sales	250				
			January 21	Sales returns		50
January 29	Sales	350				

The content of the account tells us that on:

- January 1, AL Ltd owed us £400 – this company is a **debtor** (an **asset**) of our firm;
- January 5, our firm received a cheque from AL Ltd and paid it into the bank account – the £380 cheque pays off the balance it owed at the start of the month because we have allowed this company £20 discount (the £380 cheque plus £20 discount = the £400 balance owing);
- January 12, our firm sold goods worth £250 on credit to AL Ltd – since these are not paid for immediately, this £250 debt represents the amount owed to us by AL Ltd;
- January 21, AL Ltd has returned goods to us worth £50 – the returns, the value of which is deducted from the amount AL Ltd owes to us, may be a result of poor quality, damaged or otherwise unsuitable goods sent by us;
- January 29, we sell a further £350 to AL Ltd – this brings the total owed to us to £550.

> **Crucial concept**
>
> A **debtor** is a customer who owes money to a supplier as a result of buying goods on credit from the supplier. The supplier treats this debt (the balance owed by the debtor) as an **asset**: an asset is defined as an item **owned** by a business.

You may meet alternative ways of displaying this information: for example, a '3-column' approach that provides more information, is as follows:

AL Ltd Account

		£	£	£
January 1	Balance	400		400
January 5	Bank		380	20
	Discount		20	0
January 12	Sales	250		250
January 21	Sales returns		50	200
January 29	Sales	350		550

Notice how the first two £ columns are identical to the more traditional lay-out shown earlier. This layout has the advantage that a running balance is shown, and therefore at any time the amount owed by the customer (debt-or) can be seen.

You will meet the term **ledger** in connection with accounts, regardless of how they are displayed, or whether they are kept using manual or com-puterised systems.

Crucial concept | **Ledger** is the name given to the collection of accounts. In practice, the ledger is organised into different sections (see page 44).

We also use accounts to **interpret** financial information. For example, AL Ltd's account, as one of our debtors, will be analysed by credit control staff, checking the age of the debt owed in order to ensure that our firm is being paid regularly and that we will not have to write off the amount owed as a bad debt.

Crucial tip | Interpreting/analysing information is the key role of the accountant.

Quick check | 1. What is an 'account'?
2. Define the terms 'debtor', 'asset' and 'ledger'.

| Section 2 | Transactions and source documents |

What are you studying?

Here, we explain how transactions affect the records of a business, and where the basic information concerning these transactions is recorded. Knowing how information 'flows' through a firm will help you to understand and interpret the summaries of financial information that you will meet in the form of final accounts and statements.

How will you be assessed on this?

As with Section 1, you are not likely to be tested in depth on the informa-tion in this section, which again gives important background detail. You need to know the key business trading documents, such as sales and pur-chase invoices, and credit notes: you may also have to, at some stage, un-dertake a range of calculations (e.g. percentage discount, VAT) associated with these documents.

Firms must deal with a wide range of business **transactions**: examples include buying and selling goods on credit, paying bills, and receiving and paying cash and cheques.

A business **transaction** records the movement of value. The transaction is often recorded on a **source document** — examples include invoices, credit notes, cheques, petty cash vouchers — from which the relevant financial information for the account(s) is extracted by accounts staff.

We've already described in Section I the transactions associated with AL Ltd's account; we can now identify the relevant source documents for our firm.

- January 5 Bank £380 and Discount £20: AL Ltd's **cheque** plus **remittance advice** (sent by AL Ltd with the cheque to explain the transaction) act as the source documents from which we update AL Ltd's account.

- January 12 Sales £250: we will have despatched the goods and sent a **sales invoice**, a copy of which we use to update the relevant accounts.

- January 21 Sales returns £50: our response is to send a **credit note** to AL Ltd, advising that we are reducing the amount owed to us by the value of the goods that are returned.

- January 29 Sales £350: we send another **sales invoice** to AL Ltd.

Here are other important examples of business transactions and relevant source documents.

Example transaction	Relevant source document
We buy goods on credit from NM Ltd	*Purchase invoice*
We pay NM Ltd by cheque	*Cheque (stub)*
We pay an electricity bill by cheque	*Cheque stub; electric bill*
We use petty cash to pay for stamps	*Petty cash voucher*

 Identify possible source documents from your own experience: e.g. payslips, orders, receipts.

If you're not familiar with business documents, study the sample sales invoice shown in Figure 2.1 — the supplier is VEL and the customer Emilaur. If Emilaur doesn't take the discount offered, the amount payable is £55.31 (the VAT % must be calculated on the amount less 2½% discount). VEL will use this sales invoice as its source document for the sale: Emilaur will treat the invoice as a purchase invoice, and again extract information from it to record the value of the purchase in its own accounts.

<table>
<tr><td colspan="7" style="text-align:center">VEL Co Ltd
Hampton Road, Welshampton WV10 2ER</td></tr>
</table>

To: Emilaur Ltd Bucks Road Hadley HA11 1TY				Invoice No: S 146 Date: 16.01.01 Order No: 190881	

Product code	Quantity and description	Unit price £ p		TOTAL £ p	
EV 20	24 Blue Bear teddy bears	1	50	36	00
LS 18	12 Frisco toy dogs	2	25	27	00
				63	00
	Less: trade discount 25%			15	75
				47	25
	VAT 17½%			8	06
	TOTAL			55	31

Terms: 2½% 28 days
      E & O E   VAT Reg. 691 411

Figure 2.1 Example of a sales invoice

Crucial tip   Research the layout and content of other business documents, especially in the way they record VAT and (if relevant) discount.

Accountants often use **books of original entry** to record the trading transactions shown on these source documents:

- the **sales (day) book** collects information from the sales invoices, summarising and totalling this to obtain the value of the firm's credit sales;
- the **purchases (day) book** does the same job for the firm's credit purchases; and
- returns books will be used to record the goods being returned both by and to the firm.

Crucial concept   **Books of original** (or **prime**) **entry** are used to collect, analyse and total the information contained in source documents.

Figure 2.2 shows an abbreviated sales book, which includes the information from the invoice in Figure 2.1. (NB: The 'bears' and 'dogs' figures are each reduced by 25% trade discount.)

Date	Customer	Invoice no.	Amount £	Analysis			
				VAT £	**Bears** £	**Dogs** £	**Dolls** £
16/1	Emilaur	S 146	55.31	8.06	27.00	20.25	
17/1	Marks	S 147	105.75	15.75	35.00	25.00	30.00
	Westfields	S 148	89.89	13.39		14.50	62.00
			250.95	37.20	62.00	59.75	92.00

Figure 2.2 Extract from a sales book

Quick check
1. List **four** different source documents used in trading.
2. Describe how the accounts staff use source documents.
3. Outline the purpose of a book of original entry.

<table>
<tr><td>Section 3</td><td>Entering information into accounts</td></tr>
</table>

What are you studying?

This Section explains the mechanics of double-entry book-keeping, which underpin all financial accounting. You will study how entries in accounts are made: this links with the next Section, which shows how these accounts are balanced and what this balance means.

How will you be assessed on this?

You may be tested through being given a series of transactions to enter into accounts. Such questions are often based on constructing, balancing and interpreting accounts. At the very least, you will need to demonstrate a clear understanding of how account entries are made, and what each of the account balances means to a firm.

Every business transaction has a twofold effect: because of this, two accounts are normally affected by the transaction. One account is **debited** and the other is **credited**. AL Ltd's account on page 32 has a series of debit entries (in the left-hand section) and credit entries (on the right).

Crucial tip
You need to memorise the difference between debit and credit, and be sure not to confuse the everyday meaning of the term 'credit' with its meaning in financial accounting.

Crucial concept
A **debit** entry is made in the left-hand £ column of an account, whereas a **credit** entry is made in the right-hand £ column.

If we are given business transactions to record in accounts, we have two questions to answer:

(a) which accounts are involved?
(b) which account is debited, and which is credited?

We get the answer to (a) by identifying **which items have changed in amount/value**. For example:

Transaction	Accounts affected
(1) Employee's salary paid by cheque, £100	The value of **salaries** is affected, and the firm's **bank** balance is also affected: these are the accounts.
(2) We pay a supplier the amount we owe (£50) by cheque	The amount in our **bank** account changes, and the **supplier's** relationship with us has also changed.

 Crucial concept   Suppliers from whom we buy goods on credit are know as **creditors**.

(3) We sell goods for £25, and receive cash	The values of both our **sales** and our **cash** are affected by this transaction.

When we establish which accounts are involved in the transaction, we can answer (b), identifying which account is debited and which is credited. There are two popular methods:

Method 1   Does the account receive or give value? The rule is to **debit the account receiving value; credit the account giving value**.

Crucial tip   The 'receiving/giving' approach is easiest to apply with cash and bank transactions.

If we apply this rule to the above transactions, we have:

(1) Employee's salary paid by cheque, £100
The salary is received by the employee (also, the firm receives the value of work done by the employee), so salaries a/c is debited.

The bank has given value, so this account is credited.

(2) We pay a supplier £50 by cheque
The creditor *receives* the cheque, so the creditor's account is debited.

The bank gives value again, so it is again credited.

(3) Goods sold for cash, £25

Cash is received, so this account is debited.   Sales are given, so this a/c is credited.

Method 2   Classify the account, and apply the following rules:

Asset a/c		Liability a/c	
Debit an *increase* in value	Credit a *decrease* in value	Debit a *decrease* in value	Credit an *increase* in value

If the account represents an **expense**, it is debited. If the account represents a **revenue** (income), it is credited.

Crucial tip — You will need to memorise these rules: the first two letters of the word 'debit' remind you to **De**bit **Ex**penses, and the first two letters of 'credit' remind you to **Cr**edit **Re**venues (income).

Crucial concept — A **liability** represents something owed by a firm, such as a loan or a debt to a creditor (supplier). **Expenses** are the everyday costs a firm must meet, such as wages, advertising and delivery costs; **revenues** (or **income**) represent the gains from its trading (e.g. sales income).

Applying these rules to the transactions above:

(1) Employee's salary paid by cheque, £100

Salaries are an expense, so the account is debited. The bank account (asset) has decreased in value, so it is credited.

(2) We pay a supplier £50 by cheque

The amount we owe the supplier (liability) is decreased by this payment, so the supplier's account is debited. Again, the balance at bank (asset) falls, so this account is credited.

(3) Goods sold for cash, £25

Sales are a revenue, so this account is credited. The firm's cash (an asset) increases by the sale, so this account is debited.

Crucial tip — Practise using both methods, and you can then select the one you are more comfortable with.

Quick check

1. Define these four main types of accounts: assets, liabilities, expenses, revenues.
2. Study AL Ltd's account shown on page 32 and answer these questions:
   (a) Is AL Ltd a debtor or creditor?
   (b) Explain why the account was (i) debited on the 12th, and
       (ii) credited on the 21st.

Section 4 — Account balances and types

What are you studying?

This Section describes how accounts are balanced, and what these balances mean in practice. It also explains the difference between two types of expenditure, and why this difference is important.

How will you be assessed on this?

You will be given a series of account balances, either in the form of a trial balance, or as final accounts. Questions based on a trial balance often ask you to construct final accounts from this information: to do so successfully requires an understanding of what each balance means. Those questions based on final accounts require you to interpret the information: again, this relies on your knowledge of the nature of these balances and how they arise.

When you total the two sides of an account, you will probably find that these totals are different. In such a case, an account is said to have a **balance**.

Crucial concept

An account **balance** is the difference between the totals of its debit and credit sides.

Balances are of two kinds: debit and credit. An account is said to have a debit (Dr) balance if its debit total is greater than its credit total; it has a credit (Cr) balance if its credit total is greater than its debit total.

Sometimes, you are given a list of balances, and not told whether they are debit or credit ones. Of the account types we have studied so far, there is an easy way to remember whether the account will have a debit or a credit balance: the word 'EARL'.

Dr	**Cr**
E(xpenses)	
A(ssets)	
	R(evenues)
	L(iabilities)

If you can identify the account as either an expense or an asset, you know that the balance is a debit one; if the account is either a revenue or a liability, it will have a credit balance.

AL Ltd's account from page 32 is copied below. The debit side totals £1,000 and the credit side totals £450: this account therefore has a **debit balance** of £550. We enter the balance as shown, recording it first on the smaller side (so the totals – £1,000 in this case – can be entered and the account 'ruled off') and then bringing it down to its 'correct', debit, side.

AL Ltd Account

		£			£
January 1	Balance	400			
			January 5	Bank	380
				Discount	20
January 12	Sales	250			
			January 21	Sales returns	50
January 29	Sales	350			
			January 31	**Balance c/d**	**550**
		1,000			1,000
February 1	**Balance b/d**	**550**			

Why is it important to know what these balances represent? If we return to our fourfold classification of accounts, we can regroup them using how they affect a firm's **final accounts**.

Crucial concept The term **final accounts** refers to a firm's profit and loss account, which shows the profit (or loss) made in the financial period, and its balance sheet – a statement of its financial position.

Expenses and **R**evenues   go to the ⟶   Profit & Loss account

Assets and **L**iabilities   go to the ⟶   Balance Sheet

(We study these final accounts in depth later.)

Crucial tip It is particularly important to classify these balances correctly.

A problem arises if we classify the accounts incorrectly. The account balances shown in the profit and loss account represent the firm's **revenue expenditure**, whereas the accounts listed in the balance sheet represent the firm's **capital expenditure**.

Crucial concept

The term **revenue expenditure** refers to a firm's normal running expenses; **capital expenditure** occurs when a firm buys (or improves) **fixed assets** (long-lasting assets such as buildings, equipment, vehicles).

If we wrongly record revenue expenditure as capital expenditure, this means that we will be **understating our expenses**, and therefore **overstating our profit** because

Profit = Revenue less Expenses

If, therefore, we categorise capital expenditure as revenue expenditure, we are charging too much expense and thus **understating our profit**.

Crucial tip

A difficulty you will face is when we '**capitalise**' revenue expenditure: a firm can treat expenses associated with buying fixed assets (e.g. wages paid to install equipment, or legal fees arising from buying property) as capital expenditure, and add them to the value of the fixed asset.

Quick check

1. Calculate and enter the balance on this account.

Sales account

		£
February 7	Cash sales	236
February 14	Cash sales	186
February 21	Cash sales	301
February 28	Cash sales	156

2. How do we know whether to name a balance as 'debit' or 'credit'?

3. Which of these is revenue expenditure?

   (a) Paying petrol for sales staff cars

   (b) Buying new cars for the sales team

   (c) Servicing these cars

   (d) Building a new extension for the sales team to work in.

Section 5	The importance of timing

What are you studying?

In this Section, we introduce a key concept of financial accounting. Accountants have to obey a series of 'laws' or rules, the most fundamental of which makes them establish the difference between the profits made and the cash flow associated with these profits.

How will you be assessed on this?	Questions on this 'accruals concept' tend to fall into two categories. The easier question type asks you to describe or explain this concept, and possibly to give an example of how it works in practice. The more demanding accounts questions are built around this concept, requiring you to apply your understanding of it when calculating various amounts such as net profit.

When preparing final accounts and other financial statements, accountants are obliged to follow a series of rules. Some of these rules are as a result of laws passed (primarily the **1985 Companies Act**); others have been developed by accountants themselves, either in the form of accounting concepts or through the Accounting Standards Board which issues **Financial Reporting Standards** (FRSs). We introduce the key concepts and FRSs as you study the relevant content, and Chapter 6 summarises these.

Let's look again at AL Ltd's account. We know this company is a debtor because it is buying goods and not paying for them immediately. At the end of January, AL Ltd owed £550 for sales we made in January – £250 less £50 returns, then another £350 – and since this is owed, we have clearly not received the money for these sales. If we assume that AL Ltd pays for them in February, we have a dilemma: if we are calculating our profit for January, do we record these sales or do we treat them as occurring in February (i.e. when the cash is received)?

In English law, a sale is made when legal title to the goods passes to the buyer: e.g. when the delivery is received and signed for by AL Ltd.

Accountants follow this principle, and accept that the sales – and therefore the profit from them – take place in January. This is an example of the **accruals concept**, also known in financial accounting as the **'matching' concept**.

Crucial concept | The **accruals**, or **matching**, **concept** requires accountants to match the firm's expenses and revenues to the period to which they relate.

'Matching' is the more straightforward name for non-accountants, since what is happening is that expenses and revenues have to be matched against the financial time periods to which they refer. In the above illustration, the sales occur and the profit is regarded as being made in January, even though the cash is not received until February, the next financial period.

Credit sales are a good way for you to explain how the profit figure of a firm will differ from its cash figure.

Here's another illustration: assume on January 1 we start renting premises, the annual rent being £12,000 payable quarterly in advance. In this calendar (and financial) year, we pay the rent from our bank account on January 1, March 30, July 1, September 30 and December 31 (for the first quarter next year).

Step 1 in constructing the account is to enter the amounts **paid** throughout the year into the account – you will therefore see five entries on the debit side.

Rent A/c

		£
January 1	Bank a/c	3,000
March 30	Bank a/c	3,000
July 1	Bank a/c	3,000
September 30	Bank a/c	3,000
December 31	Bank a/c	3,000

We apply the accruals concept in matching the expense of rent to the year: this means we must show the true cost of rent £12,000, regardless of the fact we actually paid £15,000 in the year.

Step 2 is to show the amount that **should have been paid** during the year (this is transferred to the profit and loss account as an expense).

Rent A/c

		£			£
January 1	Bank a/c	3,000	December 31	Profit and loss	12,000
March 30	Bank a/c	3,000			
July 1	Bank a/c	3,000			
September 30	Bank a/c	3,000			
December 31	Bank a/c	3,000			

Step 3 is to calculate any balance on the account: in this case, the balance represents the **difference** between what has been paid and what should have been paid in the year.

Rent A/c

		£			£
January 1	Bank a/c	3,000	December 31	Profit and loss	12,000
March 30	Bank a/c	3,000			
July 1	Bank a/c	3,000			
September 30	Bank a/c	3,000	December 31	Balance carried	
December 31	Bank a/c	3,000		down	3,000
		15,000			15,000
January 1	Balance brought down	3,000			

Note that this is a debit balance, because the debit side totals more than the credit side. 'EARL' (page 39) teaches us that expenses and assets have debit balances: even though rent is an expense, the fact that on January 1 we have paid three months' rent in advance means the firm will show this **£3,000 balance as an asset**. The reason is that the firm has paid for something it has not yet received the benefit of (i.e. a quarter's rent).

Similarly, if the firm owes money for, say, power at the end of the financial period, the amount owed is an **accrual** and is treated as a liability (remember the definition of a liability is something that is owed by a business). Here, the firm will again record the true cost of power as an expense and charge it against its profit, and will show the amount still owed as a liability.

Crucial concept   A **prepayment** refers to an amount paid in advance; an **accrual** is when the item is still owing.

Crucial tip   When you study final accounts (Chapter 3), you will see prepaid expenses shown as assets, and accrued expenses shown as liabilities.

Quick check   1. What is the difference between the 'accruals concept' and an 'accrual'?

2. A firm has prepaid rates at the end of its financial year. Is this an asset or a liability?

Section 6   Division of the ledger

What are you studying?   Accountants organise, and try to keep too much detail out of, the ledger accounts. You will study how and why they separate these accounts into different ledgers.

How will you be assessed on this?   It is likely that you will be tested on your knowledge of control accounts (see page 59), which are created as a result of dividing up the ledger.

We know from our everyday lives that we need to look after and organise our own money and other assets. This is no different for a business: simply having accounts indicates that value exists in the business, and this value – in the form of money and other assets – must be **organised** and **controlled**.

The first important area to control is that of money, whether literally cash or whether in the form of a business bank account. Firms therefore normally keep separate all the accounts dealing with cash and cheques. A firm's **cash book** contains all cash records – accounts – which may include petty cash and will certainly include a business bank account.

Another important area for analysis and control involves credit transactions. Firms create a **sales ledger**, which will contain all debtor accounts. This enables the accountant (or the credit control staff) to analyse the age of the various debts, and to take appropriate action to chase up money owed. We can also logically group together the firm's creditors in a **purchase ledger**, analysis of which will show the total amount that our firm owes to its credit suppliers.

All other accounts – the remaining assets and liabilities, and expense and revenue accounts – can be kept together in a **general** (or **nominal**) **ledger**. In practice, this **main ledger** may be subdivided, e.g. a **private ledger** may be kept, containing the more private accounts such as the final accounts and the capital account of a sole trader.

You are now in a position to see that accountants use the terms 'Sales' and 'Purchases' in different contexts:

Sales **account** Purchases **account**	These are accounts in the general ledger (not the sales or purchases ledgers!) to record sales and purchases of goods
Sales **day book** Purchases **day book**	These record information from source documents (invoices) that contain details of sales and purchases made on credit. The totals are posted to the sales and purchases accounts
Sales **ledger** Purchases **ledger**	These are groupings of debtor and creditor accounts (and do not contain the sales and purchases accounts!).

 Crucial tip — This analysis is important, so study carefully the above details.

 Quick check

1. Why are accounts recording cash and cheques kept separate from the other accounts?
2. What is kept in (a) a sales ledger; (b) a sales (day) book?

Crucial examples

1. For each transaction, state which account you would debit, and which you would credit.

	Dr	Cr
Paid wages in cash	....	....
Bought goods on credit from Palmer	....	....
Received a cheque from Edwards	....	....
Sold goods for cash	....	....

2. Explain each entry in the following ledgers and accounts.

(a) Purchases ledger

G. Fitzpatrick Account		Dr	Cr	Balance
		£	£	£
August 1	Balance			1,600
11	Purchases		1,360	2,960
14	Returns	80		2,880
18	Bank	1,560		
	Discount	40		1,280
24	Purchases		400	1,680

(b) General ledger   Business rates account

		£			£
January 1	Balance	200			
July 2	Bank a/c	3,600			
December 31	Balance c/d	200			
		4,000			4,000
			January 1	Balance b/d	200

3. Write in the spaces below whether the following transactions are capital or revenue expenditure.

   (a) Purchase of motor vehicle   ....

   (b) Annual insurance on motor vehicle ....

   (c) Cost of rebuilding factory wall   ....

   (d) Purchase of freehold land   ....

   (e) Legal costs on acquiring the land   ....

   (f) Repainting factory   ....

   (g) Repairing factory roof   ....

4. Explain each of these terms:

Account	Expense
Accrual	Final accounts
Accruals concept	Income (revenue)
Asset	Ledger
Balance	Liability
Book of original entry	Matching concept
Capital expenditure	Prepayment
Creditor	Revenue expenditure
Debit and credit	Source document
Debtor	Transaction

Answers

		Dr	**Cr**
1.	Paid wages in cash	wages	cash
	Bought goods on credit from Palmer	purchases	Palmer
	Received a cheque from Edwards	bank	Edwards
	Sold goods for cash	cash	sales

2. (a) Fitzpatrick:

　1: balance owing to Fitzpatrick (a creditor, since the account is in the purchases ledger).

　11: purchases from Fitzpatrick, which increases the amount owed to this firm.

　14: return of goods to Fitzpatrick, reducing the balance owed.

　18: payment to Fitzpatrick for goods originally costing £1,600 (£40 discount).

　24: more goods bought, leaving £1,680 owing to the creditor at the end of the month.

(b) Business rates:

　January 1: opening balance of rates paid in advance – a debit (asset) balance.

　July 2: cheque paid for business rates.

　December 31: closing balance – a credit balance (it is brought down to the credit side on January 1), which represents rates owing at the end of the year (an accrual).

3. Revenue expenditure – normal costs of running the business – are (b), (c), (f) and (g). The other items involve acquiring or improving assets, including (e) which is an example of capitalising revenue expenditure.

4. Check your answers against the **Crucial concepts** in the chapter.

Crucial reading and research

Reading

These books provide more information on the background to double entry:

Dodge, R. (1997) *Foundations of Business Accounting*, 2nd edn. International Thomson Business Press (ISBN 1 86512 153 7). See Chapter 2, 'The basis of financial statements', and Chapter 3, 'The basic double-entry system'.

Dyson, J. R. (1994) *Accounting for Non-Accounting Students*, 3rd edn. Pitman Publishing (ISBN 0 273 60435 X). See Chapter 3, 'Recording accounting information': basic double entry (pp. 41–52).

Wood, F. and Sangster, A. (1999) *Business Accounting 1*, 8th edn. Financial Times/Pitman Publishing (ISBN 0 273 63742 8). See Part 1, 'Introduction to double entry', Chapters 1–5.

Research

In the last chapter I suggested that, for appropriate research, you obtain some published accounts from limited companies. Having now studied the nature of basic double-entry, you will find that these published accounts tend to group the various expense, revenue, asset and liability accounts together.

Study the notes that accompany these accounts, in particular how the various expenses and assets are grouped together to obtain the final totals.

CHAPTER 3

PREPARING FOR
FINAL ACCOUNTS

Chapter summary

This Chapter provides the setting for the financial statements you will meet later in the book. It introduces you to a simple trial balance, explains how errors are corrected, and illustrates the workings of control accounts and bank reconciliation statements.

Studying this Chapter will help you to:

- appreciate how a basic trial balance is constructed;

- distinguish between, and correct, errors in ledger accounts; and

- explain how sales ledger and purchases ledger control accounts function.

Assessment targets

Target 1: constructing a simple trial balance

In your assessment, you may be given a series of balances to organise in the form of a trial balance. Exercise 1 at the end of the Chapter assesses your ability to do this.

Target 2: correcting errors that do not affect the balancing of the trial balance

You will need to understand the different types of errors that can be made. Exercise 2 at the end of the Chapter tests your ability to identify those errors where debit still equals credit.

Target 3: correcting errors that will affect the trial balance balancing

You may also be required to correct errors where debit does not equal credit. Exercise 3 at the end of the Chapter tests you on this.

Target 4: constructing control accounts

In your studies you will meet the use of control accounts, particularly those affecting the sales and purchases ledgers. Exercise 4 at the end of the Chapter assesses whether you can construct appropriate control accounts.

Target 5: undertaking bank reconciliation

You may be asked to reconcile – agree – two sets of records relating to a company's bank balance. Exercise 5 at the end of the Chapter tests your ability to reconcile the two figures.

Target 6: using accounting terms appropriately

Throughout your assessments, you will have to use accounting terms appropriately. Exercise 6 at the end of the Chapter assesses whether you can define these terms with ease.

Crucial concepts

These are the key terms and concepts you will meet in this Chapter:

accounting equation	Journal
'as at'	Overcast/overstated
Bank reconciliation	Profit
Bank reconciliation statement	Suspense account
$C = A - L$	Undercast/understated
Control account	Unpresented cheques

Relevant links

In Chapter 4 you'll use your knowledge of simple trial balances when constructing final accounts. You also apply your understanding of double entry (from Chapter 2) in this chapter, and you'll need to be familiar with control and suspense accounts when studying the information and questions in the chapters on final accounts (Chapters 4–6).

Section I	The trial balance

What are you studying?

We start by studying the trial balance. You will find that it serves three main purposes:

- to check the accuracy of the transactions entered in the accounts;
- to obtain a balance on each account; and
- to provide information needed for the final accounts.

How will you be assessed on this?

Although you may be asked to explain the purpose of a trial balance, or possibly construct one from a series of account balances, you will usually be given a completed trial balance and be asked to use it for constructing final accounts. This is an extremely popular way to assess your understanding of the trial balance. It is likely that you will be given a series of notes that accompany the trial balance (such as the various accruals or prepayments explained in the last chapter), and be expected to adjust the figures accordingly.

In the last Chapter, we studied how accounts were constructed. Many of these accounts have **balances**: in other words, the total of one side (debit or credit) was larger than the total of the other side.

Since the main feature of double-entry book-keeping is that **for every debit there is a credit**, the total debits should equal the total credits. Balancing accounts calculates the 'net' debit or credit, and so the total of all the debit balances must equal the total of all the credit balances.

Here is a list of balances for a business, taken on 30 June. How are they constructed into a trial balance?

 Crucial tip If you can recall 'EARL' from the last Chapter, you can apply it to help you solve the nature of most balances.

	£		£
Purchases	10,000	Discounts received	450
Sales	16,000	Discounts allowed	400
Opening stock	2,000	Carriage on sales	300
Salaries	1,500	Bank	3,000
Vehicles	4,000	Machinery	3,500
Debtors	3,400	Advertising	300
Creditors	2,300	Bad debts	350

The end result is shown below. (I have recorded E, A, R or L by the relevant item as a reference.) Notice the wording of the heading: the trial balance is always **'as at'** rather than 'for the period ending'.

You may be given a list of balances with 'capital' omitted: this can be calculated from the difference between the debit and credit totals.

Trial balance as at 30 June

		£	£
E	Purchases	10,000	
R	Sales		16,000
A	Opening stock	2,000	
E	Salaries	1,500	
A	Vehicles	4,000	
A	Debtors	3,400	
L	Creditors		2,300
R	Discounts received		450
E	Discounts allowed	400	
E	Carriage on sales	300	
A	Bank	3,000	
A	Machinery	3,500	
E	Advertising	300	
E	Bad debts	350	
L	**Capital**		**10,000**
		28,750	28,750

 Crucial tip   Closing stock never goes in the trial balance; it is shown as a note underneath the trial balance.

Crucial concept   The accounting equation **Capital = Assets − Liabilities** can be
applied to the trial balance, for example in calculating the capital balance.

The trial balance has a rather limited role. Although it will indicate that
some errors (mainly arithmetical ones) have been made, it will not help
identify all types of errors (see page 53).

 Crucial tip   The trial balance, like the balance sheet, is not an account 'proper'; it
does not form part of double entry.

 Quick check   1. Describe the **three** main purposes of a trial balance.
2. Why is the heading of a trial balance 'as at' rather than 'for period
ending'?

Section 2   Correcting errors (I)

What are you studying?

We need to examine the limitations of the trial balance in greater depth. Its main limitation is that it only provides an arithmetical check of the accuracy of 'the books'. Here, we learn about one category of errors that will not be revealed through constructing a trial balance.

How will you be assessed on this?

You may be given a series of errors and asked to identify them by name, and/or by whether they affect the balancing of the trial balance. The more awkward questions give you the account details, and ask you to correct the errors. An additional twist occurs when the question asks you to show how the firm's profit figure is (or is not) affected by each of these errors.

....

We know from the last Section that the trial balance serves as an arithmetical check only. As an example, the trial balance will not identify whether the correct accounts have been used, simply whether one account has been debited and another credited for the same amount.

Errors not affecting the balancing of the trial balance

The errors not disclosed by the trial balance occur in situations where the debit entry or total matches the credit entry or total. There are six types of errors found, and you need to know their nature in order to answer questions on how they are corrected.

Many students find this a very difficult topic, so here's a summary of the six, with examples.

Crucial tip	The initials 'COR COP' will help you remember these six errors.

Name	Description	Example
COMMISSION	Wrong **personal** account is used, e.g. wrong debtor	*'Sold goods to J. Jones £50'* Sales account | 50 F. Jones account 50 |
OMISSION	Transaction omitted completely omitted from the ledger, i.e. omitted from **both** accounts	*'Cash sales £10'* Sales account Cash account

REVERSAL The account that should be debited is credited, and vice versa

'Cash sales, £10'

Sales account

| 10 | |

Cash account

| | 10 |

COMPENSATING Errors that cancel each other out, e.g. debit balance £10 too much, another debit balance £10 too little

Rent payable account

20	
20	
50	

Advertising account

20	
20	
30	

ORIGINAL ENTRY The original amount is entered incorrectly in **both** accounts

'Cash sales, £10'

Cash account

| 100 | |

Sales account

| | 100 |

PRINCIPLE The wrong **class** of account is used, e.g. expense debited to an asset account

'Paid motor expenses £400'

Motor vehicles account

| 400 | |

Bank account

| | 400 |

 Crucial tip Remember, the balancing of the trial balance is not affected by any of these errors because, in all cases, **DEBIT = CREDIT.**

Correcting the errors

Accountants use the **journal** as a record of the entries they make. You will meet the journal throughout your studies, particularly when errors need correcting.

Crucial concept The **journal** acts as a book of original entry to summarise the key entries made in the accounts.

The journal layout is quite simple: the account to be debited is recorded, then the account to be credited, then a **narrative** summary of the transaction is made.

 Crucial tip — Often, you are not required to provide a narrative in exam questions involving the journal.

With errors, the key point is to **make sure you identify the type of error**: is it one that affects the trial balance balancing, or not? Establishing this indicates whether or not a **suspense account** will need to be used.

 Crucial concept — The **suspense account** is used to help correct errors where debit **does not** equal credit. It is not used for the six errors where debit equals credit.

Remember: the 'COR COP' errors are **not** disclosed by the trial balance. The six errors illustrated above would be corrected as shown below (the correcting double entry is ringed).

Crucial tip — To correct these errors we need to identify:
(a) what **has** happened; and
(b) what **should have** happened.

1. Commission: 'Sold goods to J. Jones, £50'

What **has** happened is that the entry is in the wrong account (F. Jones): it must be cancelled by making a credit entry. What **should have** happened is that the entry should be in J. Jones's account, so it is now entered in – debited to – this account.

F. Jones a/c		J. Jones a/c	
50	(50)	(50)	

2. Omission: 'Cash sales, £10'

What has happened is that both entries have been omitted, so simply enter the transaction.

Cash a/c		Sales a/c	
(10)			(10)

3. Reversal: 'Cash sales, £10'

Here, what has happened is that each account has the entry on the wrong side. To correct, enter **double** the amount (using the same amount will only cancel the incorrect figure) in the accounts.

Cash a/c		Sales a/c	
20	10	10	20

4. Compensating (errors of addition cancelling each other)

What has happened is that the rent payable account totals £10 too much, and the advertising account £10 too little. The errors can be corrected by adjusting the balances as shown.

Rent payable a/c		Advertising a/c	
50	10	30	
		10	

5. Original entry: 'Cash sales, £10'

What has happened is that the original figure is incorrectly shown as £100, and needs reducing to £10 by making an adjusting entry on the other side of the accounts.

Cash a/c		Sales a/c	
100	90	90	100

6. Principle: 'Paid motor expenses, £400'

What has happened is that a wrong class of account has been used. To correct, remove and post to the correct account.

Motor vehicles a/c		Motor expenses a/c	
400	400	400	

The journal record showing the correction of these errors would in fact be created before the double entry was carried out: using the first correction, we have:

Journal

(Date)		£	£
	J. Jones a/c	50	
	F. Jones a/c		50
	Being correction of posting		
	to wrong debtor account		

Crucial tip   Double-check that the journal debits and credits match the debits and credits in the various accounts.

Quick check
1. List and describe the 'COR COP' errors.
2. With these errors, will debit still equal credit?
3. If a posting is made to the correct class of account and on the correct side, but in the wrong account, is it an error of:
   (a) omission
   (b) principle
   (c) commission
   (d) compensation?
4. Complete the journal entries for the other five errors that are corrected above.

Section 3 — Correcting errors (2)

What are you studying?

The strength of the trial balance is that it provides an arithmetical check of the accuracy of the accounts. Here, we study the type of errors that **will** be revealed through constructing a trial balance, and how they are corrected.

How will you be assessed on this?

The question may list a series of errors and ask you to name them, and/or state whether they affect the balancing of the trial balance. The more challenging questions make you correct these errors. As with the other type of error in Section 2, the question may require you to correct a given profit figure.

The errors described below will stop the trial balance from balancing, because here we find that **debit ≠ credit**. The trial balance is unlikely to disclose exactly where the error lies: it simply doesn't balance, and therefore draws attention to the fact that the ledger contains at least one error:

- in the accounts:
  - only a single entry has been made;
  - double entry is inaccurate (different figures recorded in the two accounts);
  - the transaction has resulted in two debit (or two credit) entries;
  - a figure has been posted incorrectly to one account.

- in the trial balance itself:
  - a balance may be entered on the wrong side of the trial balance;
  - an account balance may have been omitted from the list of balances;
  - there may be an error in totalling the trial balance columns.

Crucial tip   Always check: with the error, does debit = credit?

We've already defined the suspense account in Section 2. This account is created to make the totals of the trial balance agree. If, for example, the debit column total of the trial balance is greater than the credit column total, suspense will have a **credit** balance equalling this difference (to make the totals agree).

Since the trial balance does not agree, debit does not equal credit. The error is corrected (a single account is normally involved), and the other entry is made in suspense. For example:

'Purchased goods by cheque, £150'	Purchases account		Bank account	
	150			15

Here, debit and credit totals do not agree: the trial balance won't balance. Its debit total will be £135 greater than its credit total, so suspense will have a credit balance of £135.

To correct this error we credit the bank account with £135 and record the other entry in suspense (i.e. a debit of £135, which will cancel the credit balance).

Errors and net profit

Crucial concept   **Profit** is the difference between revenues and expenses.

You may be asked to correct a given profit figure, which is incorrect due to a number of errors. Assets and liabilities tend not to affect profit calculations, so errors in these accounts are ignored when adjusting profit.

Crucial tip   The stock account (an asset) features in profit calculation (i.e. opening stock), so an error that involves the stock figure may affect the accuracy of the stated profit.

We must calculate whether an error has resulted in the expense or revenue being understated or overstated.

Crucial concept   **'Understated' or 'undercast'** = too little: **'overstated' or 'overcast'** = too much.

Error		Effect on profit?		Action: we must . . .
Expense is overstated	⟶	profit is understated	⟶	increase the profit figure.
Expense is understated	⟶	profit is overstated	⟶	reduce the profit figure.
Revenue is overstated	⟶	profit is overstated	⟶	reduce the profit figure.
Revenue is understated	⟶	profit is understated	⟶	increase the profit figure.

Quick check

1. If a trial balance's columns total £54,400 dr and £54,600 cr:
   (a) the suspense account will have a balance of how much?
   (b) will this balance be dr or cr?

2. How would the error corrected above (the £150 transaction) be shown in the journal?

Section 4 — Control accounts

What are you studying?

Many transactions in accounts involve purchases and sales. Control accounts can be used to summarise a firm's credit sales and credit purchases. In this Section, we outline the principles on which sales and purchase ledger control accounts are based. You will learn why these accounts exist, and how they are constructed.

How will you be assessed on this?

Questions on control accounts give the assessor the chance to test your knowledge of how they are constructed and used. One type of question provides a list of balances, and asks you to construct the relevant control account(s). Another type provides information from the books of original entry, and expects you to post this information to the various (control and other) accounts in the different ledgers.

The main control accounts you are likely to meet are the sales and purchase ledger (total debtors and total creditors) control accounts. These are based on buying and selling on credit, the division of the ledger (see page 44), and the use of books of original entry (page 35) – see Figure 3.1.

Crucial tip

You also need to revise the difference between sales and purchases **accounts**, **books** and **ledgers**.

Control accounts for the sales ledger (SL) and purchase ledger (PL) are based on the principle that the two aspects of a credit sale/purchase are recorded:

- once **in** the SL or PL; and
- once **outside** this ledger.

SL and PL control accounts are based on **totals**. We can use the SL to illustrate this:

- total credit sales can be obtained from the total of the sales day book;
- total returns from customers come from the sales returns (returns inwards) book;
- the cash book columns give us total payments from debtors, plus the associated discount;
- bad debts can be arrived at from the journal; and so on.

Each of these totals is posted once to the relevant account – sales, sales returns, bank, discount allowed, bad debts – and the other entry is made in the SL control account. The opening balance of the SL control account is arrived at by totalling the amounts owed by the individual debtors; the closing balance can now be found.

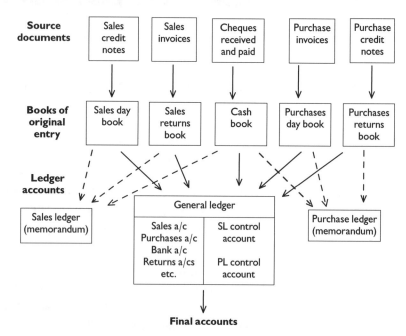

Figure 3.1 The basics of control accounts

The SL (and the PL) control account is kept in the general (nominal or main) ledger: as stated above, it 'controls' the sales ledger, and **it forms part of the double-entry system**.

 Crucial tip   The SL and PL control accounts look exactly like individual debtor and creditor accounts.

Here's an example of how to construct basic control accounts: to construct it, we must answer two questions:

- Are sales or purchases involved? (i.e. which control account?)
- Is the debtor/creditor giving or receiving value? (i.e. which side?)

(Note that you can apply the other double-entry rule: if the asset [debtor] increases in value, debit … etc.)

Opening balances: SL control £25,160; PL control £26,360

Purchases day book total	£126,300	Purchases: creditor gives = cr PL control
Sales day book total	£279,280	Sales: debtor receives = dr SL control
Cash book payments to suppliers	£119,680	Purchases: creditor receives = dr PL control
Cash book receipts from customers	£256,390	Sales: debtor gives = cr SL control
Discounts allowed	£2,320	*Sales: linked to debtor giving (cheque)
Discounts received	£1,960	*Purchases: linked to creditor receiving
Returns inwards book total	£14,600	Sales returned: debtor gives = cr SL control
Returns outwards book total	£3,570	Purchases returned: creditor receives = dr PL control
Bad debts written off	£2,100	Sales: asset of debtor (dr balance) cancelled, so cr SL control

(* with discount, always record it in the account on the same side as the cash/bank transaction)

SL control account

	£		£
Balance	25,160	Cash book	256,390
Sales	279,280	Discount allowed	2,320
		Returns in	14,600
		Bad debts	2,100
		Balance c/d	**19,030**
	304,440		304,440

PL control account

	£		£
Cash	119,680	Balance	26,360
Discount received	1,960	Purchases	126,300
Returns out	3,570		
Balance c/d	**27,450**		
	152,660		152,660

 Crucial tip — The closing balance on SL and PL control accounts represent total debtors and creditors respectively.

What about the sales and purchase ledgers? We know that these ledgers contains all debtor and creditor accounts. With a control account system, these 'accounts' **do not** form part of the double-entry system, even though they look like 'proper' accounts. They are now simply **memorandum records** of individual debtors and creditors, these records often being referred to as memorandum accounts (see Figure 3.1).

The total of the individual closing balances must equal the closing balance of the control accounts. If so, there seems to be no error in recording credit sales/purchases and related transactions; if not, there is an error in the records.

 Crucial tip | If the error affects the debtor/creditor record only, it will not affect (so will not be entered in) the control account.

Here are examples of errors affecting the individual (or totals of the) customer/supplier records **only**:

Error	Correction
Goods £2,500 sold to James omitted from this account	Dr £2,500 to James a/c
Credit side of Brown's account (supplier) £100 undercast	Add £100 to credit side of Brown a/c
Discount received £24 credited to Crosby's a/c	Dr Crosby a/c £48 (with twice the amount)
Bank payment £368 to Singh omitted from this a/c	Dr Singh a/c £368

 Quick check
1. Identify the main books of original entry used in constructing SL and PL control accounts.
2. When a firm keeps SL and PL control accounts in its general (main) ledger, what status do the sales and purchase ledgers have?

Section 5 — Bank reconciliation

What are you studying?

We can see the debtor–creditor relationship between a business and its bank from two records: the business's own bank account, and the bank statement sent by the bank to the business. Because of the timing differences, there are likely to be differences between what the business has recorded as its balance at bank, and the balance shown on the bank statement. We have to make the two balances agree by **reconciling** them.

How will you be assessed on this?

Questions on bank reconciliation provide you with these two records: what you then have to do is to account for the differences between them, and 'prove' these differences by constructing a reconciliation statement.

Crucial concept | Bank reconciliation is undertaken to ensure there are no errors relating to the firm's bank account.

The debtor–creditor relationship complicates things: for example, if the business has money in its bank account:

- the bank is its **debtor**, owing it the amount of the balance in the account
- it is the bank's **creditor** since it is owed money by the bank.

The reason why this makes things complicated is that, when we compare the two records, we find that **a debit in our (business) bank account is a credit on the bank statement, and vice versa.**

Procedure for reconciliation

What we normally find is that the two records are incomplete:

● there are items on the bank statement not recorded in our bank account; and

● there are items in our bank account not on the bank statement.

The procedure is to update our bank account with the items missing from it, and then do the reverse by updating the bank statement with those items not on it: to do this latter updating, we construct a bank reconciliation statement.

> Crucial concept
>
> A **bank reconciliation statement** is constructed in order to agree the two balances: the bank balance in the firm's books, and the balance on the bank statement.

1. Identify those items on the statement which are not as yet recorded in the bank account.
2. Work out whether the item will increase or reduce the balance at bank: if it increases the bank balance (it is a credit on the statement), debit it in the bank account; if it reduces the balance at bank (a debit on the statement), credit it to the account.
3. Calculate the updated bank account balance.
4. Create the bank reconciliation statement ('as at' the closing date) by first recording the closing balance on the statement.
5. Identify items not on the statement but in our bank account.
6. If the item has increased our balance at bank (i.e. a debit in the account), add it to the bank statement balance; if it has reduced our bank balance (a credit in the account), deduct it from the statement.
7. The closing balance should now equal the updated bank account balance: if it does not, there will be an error in one (or both) of the records.

Exercise 5 at the end of this Chapter is on bank reconciliation, and applies the steps explained above. You'll see it uses a bank reconciliation statement layout essentially as follows:

Bank reconciliation statement as at…	£
Balance as per bank statement	x
Add cheques not yet paid into bank	x
	xx
Less unpresented cheques	(x)
Balance as per updated bank account	xx

Crucial concept — The term unpresented cheques refers to cheques (e.g. sent to suppliers) which have not been presented to our bank for payment, i.e. have not been deducted from our bank balance.

 Crucial tip — Make sure you check carefully whether either record shows an overdrawn balance.

If you are given overdrawn figures you can still use the same 'logic', checking whether the item reduces the overdraft (i.e. it would increase the balance at bank) or increases it (i.e. it would reduce the bank balance).

Quick check

1. Explain the difference between:
   'bank reconciliation';
   'bank statement';
   'bank reconciliation statement'.
2. List the steps involved in carrying out bank reconciliation.

Crucial examples

1. Construct a trial balance from this list of balances. The balances were taken as at 30 November. By each balance, indicate whether it is an expense, an asset, a revenue (income) or a liability.

Purchases	£14,630	Sales	£18,470	Wages	£2,200
Motor expenses	£500	Insurance	£150	Rent	£570
Vehicles	£12,500	Debtors	£3,550	Creditors	£4,580
Cash and bank	£2,460	Opening stock	£350	Closing stock	£360
Capital ?					

2. Give the journal entries necessary to correct these errors. For each error, state whether net profit is affected and, if so, what the effect is.

   (a) Sales £465 on credit to J. Harris debited to H. Harris a/c.
   (b) Cheque £95 paid to B. Sanders debited to bank a/c and credited to B. Sanders.
   (c) Bank charges £32 debited to business rates a/c.
   (d) Loan interest £600 debited to premises a/c.

3. A trial balance fails to agree by £40. Which one of the following errors could have caused this?

   • A sale of goods, £40, to M. Patel, debited in error to P. Patel's account
   • A machine sold for scrap, £40, credited to the sales account
   • A payment for insurance £40 had been debited to the rent account
   • A cheque for £20 received from L. Robbins had been debited to L. Robinson's account.

4. The following errors have been discovered. Explain their effect on (a) the PL control account; (b) purchase ledger balances.

   (i) An invoice for £545 has been entered in the purchase day book as £454.

(ii) Discount received of £35 has been omitted completely from the accounts.

(iii) A purchase of £45 has been entered on the wrong side of a supplier account.

5. Reconcile the two balances.

A firm's bank columns for May 2002 were as follows:

		£			£
May 1	Balance b/d	532.30	May 2	R. Price	93.00
7	Cash sales	200.50	4	D. Weston	17.50
10	B Gayle	62.70	16	D. Hughes	54.750
15	Cash sales	75.00	22	NPower	39.35
22	D. Bridgwater	7.18	23	M. Lucas	19.20
30	Cash sales	72.60	27	C. Winter	15.30
			29	J. Chorley	350.00
			30	BT	107.75
			31	Balance c/d	253.38
		950.28			950.28
June 1	Balance b/d	253.38			

The following bank statement for May was received:

		Dr	Cr	Balance
1	Balance			532.30
6	Cheque 353	93.00		439.30
7	Cash		200.50	639.750
7	Cheque 354	17.50		622.30
11	B. Gayle		62.70	685.00
15	Cash		75.00	760.00
22	Cheque 355	54.80		705.20
26	Cheque 357	19.20		686.00
27	Cheque 356	39.35		646.65
28	D. Bridgwater		7.18	653.83
28	Credit transfer		60.40	714.23
30	Standing order	54.10		660.13
30	Charges	9.80		650.33

6. Explain each of these terms:

Accounting equation	Journal
'as at'	Overcast/overstated
Bank reconciliation	Profit
Bank reconciliation statement	Suspense account
C = A − L	Undercast/understated
Control account	Unpresented cheques

Answers

1. **Trial balance as at 30 November**

	£	£
Purchases	14,630	
Sales		18,470
Wages	2,200	
Motor expenses	500	
Insurance	150	
Rent	570	
Vehicles	12,500	
Debtors	3,550	
Creditors		4,580
Cash and bank	2,460	
Opening stock	350	
Capital		**13,860**
	36,910	36,910

Notes: Closing stock £360

2. **Journal**

		£	£	
(a)	J. Harris	465		error of commission: no effect on
	H. Harris		465	net profit (assets only involved)
(b)	B. Sanders	190		reversal error: no effect on net
	Bank		190	profit (assets involved)
(c)	Bank charges	32		wrong expense a/c debited: no
	Business rates		32	effect on net profit
(d)	Loan interest	600		error of principle: net profit over-
	Premises		600	stated by £600 (too little expense has been charged)

3. L. Robbins has been debited (L. Robinson should have been **credited**), so – with the bank account being debited as well – the debit total will exceed the credit total by £40. In the other three cases, debit = credit, even though errors have been made, so the trial balance will still balance.

4. (i) PL control understates purchases by £91 (total is posted to control a/c), so the balance is £91 too little; no effect on individual records in the PL.
   (ii) PL control understates discount by £35, so PL control balance is overstated by £35; similar position for the relevant individual record in the purchase ledger.
   (iii) PL control not affected (error is in the purchase ledger record only); the supplier a/c understates purchases by £90, so the balance owed is also understated by £90.

5. Updated cash book (bank account):

	£		£
Balance b/d	253.38	Standing order	54.10
Credit transfer	60.40	Bank charges	9.80
		Updated balance c/d	**249.88**
	313.78		313.78

Bank reconciliation statement as at 31 May:

		£
Balance as per statement		650.33
Add cash not paid into bank		72.60
		722.93
Less unpresented cheques:	15.30	
	350.00	
	107.75	473.05
Balance as per updated cash book		**249.88**

6. Check your answers against the **Crucial concepts** in the chapter.

Crucial reading and research

Reading

These books provide more information on the trial balance, correction of errors and control accounts.

Dodge, R. (1997) *Foundations of Business Accounting*, 2nd edn. International Thomson Business Press (ISBN 1 86512 153 7). See Chapter 3, 'The basic double-entry system', trial balance (pp. 60–4); Chapter 5, 'The basic framework of the books', control accounts (pp. 115–18) and correcting errors (pp. 118–20).

Dyson, J. R. (1994) *Accounting for Non-Accounting Students*, 3rd edn. Pitman Publishing (ISBN 0 273 60435 X). See Chapter 3, 'Recording accounting information', trial balance (pp. 55–9).

Glautier, M. W. E. and Underdown, B. (1997) *Accounting Theory and Practice*, 6th edn. Pitman Publishing (ISBN 0 273 62444 X). See Chapter 8, 'Data processing and doube-entry bookkeeping', trial balance (pp. 93–4).

Wood, F. and Sangster, A. (1999) *Business Accounting 1*, 8th edn. Financial Times/Pitman Publishing (ISBN 0 273 63742 8). See Chapter 6, 'The trial balance'; Chapter 30 'Control Accounts'; Chapter 31 'Errors not affecting trial balance'; and Chapter 32, 'Suspense accounts and errors'.

Research

Control accounts are widely used in financial accounting, for example the use of a VAT control account when accounting for value added tax. Further reading and research into this topic will give you an even wider perspective on the nature of 'control' in financial accounting.

CHAPTER 4

FINAL ACCOUNTS OF A
SOLE TRADER

Chapter summary

This Chapter provides a summary of two of the financial statements (final accounts) that you will meet regularly in your course. The **profit and loss account** is used to calculate the business's net profit, and the **balance sheet** displays its assets and liabilities. At this stage of your studies, we concentrate on the final accounts of a sole trader.

Studying this Chapter will help you to:

- describe the nature of, and give examples of, accounting concepts;

- state the purpose of the trading and profit and loss accounts and balance sheet, and construct these financial statements;

- construct an extended trial balance to calculate net profit and display assets and liabilities;

- understand and use appropriately the various names, terms and structures that you will meet in connection with these final accounts.

Assessment targets

Target 1: understanding accounting concepts

In your assessment, you may be asked to explain certain accounting concepts. Exercise 1 at the end of the Chapter tests your understanding of these concepts.

Target 2: constructing trading, profit and loss accounts

You will have to use a trial balance, together with its supporting notes, to construct these final accounts. Exercise 2 at the end of the Chapter tests you on this.

Target 3: constructing balance sheets

You again use the trial balance (plus notes) to help construct balance sheets. Exercise 2 at the end of the Chapter also tests your ability to do this.

Target 4: constructing final accounts for non-profit-making organisations

Exercise 3 at the end of the Chapter tests your knowledge of how 'club accounts' are constructed.

Target 5: creating an ETB

You may be required to use an extended trial balance to create these final accounts. Section 6 contains a worked exercise that tests your ability to use the ETB correctly.

Target 6: calculating profit from incomplete records

You may have to work out a trader's profit figure from records that have been kept without using a full double-entry system. Exercise 4 at the end of the Chapter assesses you on this.

Target 7: using accounting names, terms and structures appropriately

You will have to use accounting terms appropriately, and create a suitable structure for your final accounts. Exercises 2, 3 and 5 at the end of the Chapter all test whether you can do this.

Crucial concepts

These are the key terms and concepts you will meet in this Chapter:

Accounting concepts	Net profit
Accumulated fund	Net worth
Carriage	Provision
Deficit	Receipts and payments a/c
Depreciation	Reducing balance method
Doubtful debts	Straight-line
Drawings	Subscriptions
ETB	Surplus
Gross profit	Working capital
Income and expenditure a/c	

Relevant links

In Chapters 5 and 6 we take your knowledge of basic final accounts further, showing you how partnership, limited company and other forms of final accounts are constructed.

Section I	Accounting concepts

What are you studying?

In this Section we summarise the basic 'rules' of accounting: you need to be aware of these accounting concepts when constructing final accounts. You will study a description of each concept, and also an example of how it operates.

How will you be assessed on this?

Directly, you may face an essay-style question that tests your knowledge of the fundamental concepts (e.g. those identified and defined in SSAP 2 – see below). To understand the nature and construction of financial statements, we also need to be familiar with what accounting concepts seek to do. Your exam or coursework will almost certainly include a numerical question on final accounts, and you will be tested on how these concepts influence the construction of accounts.

When preparing accounts, accountants take a number of concepts for granted. SSAP 2 (an SSAP is a **Statement of Standard Accounting Practice**) on **Disclosure of Accounting Policies** describes four concepts as **fundamental accounting concepts**. We have already studied the nature of one of these: the **accruals concept** (page 42). This concept states that revenue and expenses must be **matched** (it is also known as the 'matching' concept) against the accounting periods to which they refer. The other three are:

- the **going concern** concept;
- the **prudence** concept;
- the **consistency** concept.

(The 1985 Companies Act adds a fifth: the **separate valuation** principle.)

Crucial tip   It's worth memorising that SSAP 2 identifies these particular concepts.

Crucial concept   Accounting concepts help establish a degree of **objectivity** in financial accounting.

Going concern, prudence and consistency

- The **going concern** concept implies that the business will continue to operate for the foreseeable future. Its main significance is that the business's assets will not be valued at resale value: the related **cost** concept is therefore used when valuing these assets (at cost).

- The **prudence** concept states that where alternative accounting procedures or valuations are possible, the accountant will select the one that gives the **most cautious presentation** of the business's financial position/performance. A good illustration you can use is with stock valuation, where closing stock is always shown at its cost price (strictly, the lower of cost and NRV – **net realisable value**) rather than its selling price. To value stock at selling price would mean that the accountant is anticipating a profit, which is not being prudent: and by valuing at NRV where this is lower than the cost figure, the accountant is being prudent by anticipating a loss.

 Crucial tip   This concept is often simplified to 'never anticipate a profit; always anticipate a loss'.

- The **consistency** concept requires accountants to give similar items the same accounting treatment. Consistency is sought so that the firm's accounts can be validly compared year to year: but it's worth remembering that the consistency concept doesn't prevent a firm changing its accounting treatment of certain items, if circumstances require this change.

 Crucial tip   Use depreciation as an illustration: a new vehicle will be depreciated using the same method and rate as that used for existing vehicles.

Other important concepts
Other important concepts are listed in Table 4.1.

 Crucial tip   To help you remember these, check the initials: 3 Ss, 2 Ms, 2 other consonants ('EO'), 2 other vowels ('DH').

Crucial concept   In law, sole traders and partners are not legal entities separate from their owners: in financial accounting, they are treated as being separate (the entity concept).

 Quick check
1. Name and give an example of the four concepts identified by SSAP 2.
2. To what extent do (a) substance over form, and (b) the entity concept, reflect a difference between law and accounts?

Name	Description/example
Separate valuation	In determining the value of balance sheet assets and liabilities, each component item of the asset/liability must be determined, e.g. a separate valuation of each machine to get a total value for 'machinery'.
Substance over form	Where the legal form of a transaction differs from its real substance, accounting shows the transaction in accordance with this real substance, e.g. with assets bought using hire purchase, legal ownership is not until the final payment is made, but accounts show the asset as 'owned' from the beginning (as well as showing the amount still owing).
Stable monetary unit	The assumption is made that the value of the monetary unit (£) remains reasonably stable, e.g. this allows a fair comparison to be made from year to year.
Materiality	Only items sufficiently important (material) in amount or nature feature, e.g. time isn't wasted recording trivial items (such as waste paper bins) as fixed assets; they are written off as expenses.
Money measurement	Accounts only record items to which a monetary value can be given, e.g. quality of management/employees is ignored.
Entity	The business is regarded as an entity separate and distinct from its owner(s), e.g. use of owner's (capital, current and drawings) a/cs.
Objectivity	Accountants, and the accounts, must be objective, e.g. free from personal bias.
Duality	Every transaction has a dual effect, e.g. double-entry book-keeping.
Historical cost	Transactions are recorded at their historic (original) cost, e.g. vehicle bought for £15,000 is shown at that figure in the accounts.

Table 4.1 Other important concepts

Section 2 — The trading account

What are you studying?

Here, we explain how this account (or section of the profit and loss account) is constructed; in particular how cost of sales and stock figures are created and used in calculating gross profit.

How will you be assessed on this?

The trial balance is often used as a source of information from which the final accounts of a business are prepared. You will be expected to calculate the key figures of cost of sales and gross profit, and to use the gross profit figure as a basis for calculating net profit (see the next Section).

Crucial concept The purpose of the **trading account** is to calculate gross profit.

The basic structure of the debit side of the trading account is:

Opening stock $\longrightarrow$ what we start with
add purchases $\longrightarrow$ plus what we buy
less closing stock $\longrightarrow$ less what we finish with.

Crucial tip You can use the fact that stock is shown at cost price or NRV (page 71) in the trading account as a good illustration of the prudence concept.

You'll find that the purchases figure may have to be adjusted at least three times, through

- returns;

- carriage;

- drawings.

Returns

Using the separate valuation principle, sales and purchases are recorded in their separate books of original entry and separate accounts, at **gross value**. Returns are analysed separately, and you will be expected to deduct the correct returns.

Crucial tip The terms 'inwards' and 'outwards' in returns describe the direction of the goods: returns in originally went 'out' as sales, so are sales returns; returns out were first bought 'in', so are purchases returns.

Carriage

Crucial concept **Carriage** represents the transport costs of the firm's stock.

Carriage, like returns, is also 'inwards' and 'outwards': again, these terms refer to the direction in which the goods move (i.e. carriage in on purchases coming in, carriage out on sales leaving the firm). Although carriage outwards is associated with sales, it is treated as a profit and loss – **not** a trading – expense.

Crucial tip Carriage inwards and outwards both have debit balances (both are expenses): returns inwards has a debit balance but returns outwards has a credit balance.

Drawings

Drawings are a good illustration of the operation of the entity principle.

Crucial concept — **Drawings** occur when the owner withdraws value from the business for personal use.

Crucial tip — A common error is to deduct stock drawings from the closing stock figure, and not – as should be done – from purchases.

A typical trading account would therefore be constructed as follows (we'll use these balances):

Sales	£64,000	Returns inwards	£600
Purchases	£25,400	Returns outwards	£800
Opening stock	£3,650	Carriage inwards	£200

Notes: (a) closing stock is valued at £4,150 ; (b) the owner withdrew £300 goods for personal use (no entries have been made in the accounts).

Crucial tip — Profit (gross and net) is made over a period of time, so the account heading must reflect this.

Trading account for period ending . . .

	£	£
Sales		64,000
Returns inwards		(600)
		63,400
Less cost of sales:		
Opening stock	3,650	
Purchases*	24,500	
Less closing stock	(4,150)	24,000
Gross profit		39,400

*The purchases figure is calculated: £25,400 – £800 returns outwards + £200 carriage inwards – £300 stock drawings.

Quick check
1. Describe the structure of the debit side of the trading account.
2. Distinguish between: (a) carriage inwards; (b) carriage outwards; (c) returns inwards; (d) returns outwards.

Section 3	The profit and loss account

What are you studying?

This final account – the 'P&L' – is constructed in order to calculate the firm's net profit. You will study its layout, and learn how to adjust some of its expenses and revenues as a result of the notes you are given.

How will you be assessed on this?

As with the trading account, the trial balance tends to be used as the information source from which the P&L is prepared. The questions on P&L tend to be numerical ones, using a trial balance accompanied by a series of notes requiring adjustment. You will be tested on what to include in the account, you'll have to use an appropriate layout, and then calculate net profit accurately by making appropriate adjustments to relevant expense and revenue figures.

Crucial concept

The purpose of the **P&L** is to calculate the firm's net profit, by adding revenue (other than sales) to the gross profit figure, and by deducting the various expenses from this total.

Most of the difficulties associated with P&L accounts involve either:

● making adjustments as a result of prepayments or accruals; or

● calculating and including provisions for depreciation and doubtful debts.

Prepayments and accruals
Examiners test your understanding of the accruals concept (page 42) by giving you a series of notes accompanying the trial balance. For example:

Trial balance (extracts) for the year:	£	£
Rent	3,450	
Advertising	5,300	
Commission received		4,300

At the end of the year, rent paid in advance for next year £650; advertising bill still owing £95; commission received owing £20.

The key principle we use is: does the amount relate to the year in question? If **yes**, include it; if **no**, exclude it. Applying this principle to the above adjustments:

● Rent prepaid: included in the account but applies to next year, so **deduct.**

● Advertising owed: not included in the account but applies to this year so **add.**

● Commission received: not included in the account but applies to this year so **add**.

The figures for the P&L account are therefore:

- rent £3,450 − £650 = £2,800;
- advertising £5,300 + £95 = £5,395;
- commission received £4,300 + £20 = £4,320.

Crucial tip   If stuck, remember 'LP' and 'AA' : Less Prepaid, Add Accrued.

Always apply the logic of the accruals concept, however: the 'AA' and 'LP' summary only relates to **year-end** accruals and prepayments.

Provision for depreciation

Crucial concept   A **provision** is a liability of uncertain timing or amount.

Provisions come from applying the prudence concept. A **provision for depreciation** seeks to spread the cost of the fixed assets over their expected life. We do this by estimating the annual loss in value of the fixed asset, a final adjustment having to be made (profit or loss on the sale of the asset) when the asset is sold.

Crucial concept   **Depreciation** records the loss in value incurred by a fixed asset through depletion (e.g. mines), wear and tear, or obsolescence.

You will probably be taught two main methods of calculating depreciation:

- the **straight-line method**, using the formula:

$$\frac{\text{Original cost less Estimated residual (resale or scrap) value}}{\text{Estimated life}}$$

- the **reducing balance** method, where a fixed % is applied to the written-down value of the asset.

For example, an asset costing £1,000 and having an estimated life of four years and an estimated resale value of £100 will be depreciated at £225, each and every year, using the straight-line method. The reducing balance method would apply a fixed percentage, initially to the original cost and then to the reduced value (i.e. original cost less depreciation). If the percentage was fixed at, say, 40%, we would depreciate this asset as follows:

- end of year 1   £400 (40% of £1,000);
- end of year 2   £240 (40% of [£1,000 − £400]);
- end of year 3   £144 (40% of [£1,000 − £400 − £240]).

These examples serve to illustrate that the names 'straight line' and 'redu-cing balance' are derived from the amounts of depreciation calculated by each method.

Crucial concept The **reducing balance method** may result in a more realistic depre-ciation, since many fixed assets (e.g. vehicles) lose a higher percentage of their value in their early years.

Like prepayments and accruals, provision adjustments are also normally shown as notes accompanying the trial balance.

- With the depreciation provision:
  - the depreciation for the period is shown in the P&L;
  - total depreciation is shown in the balance sheet (see next Section).

For example, if the balance in the vehicles account is £36,000, the existing depreciation provision balance is £22,000 and depreciation is calculated on the reducing balance method at 25%, this year's charge for P&L will be £3,500 (25% of £14,000).

Provision for doubtful debts

Crucial concept A **provision for doubtful debts** seeks to reduce year-end debtors to a fair value on the argument that the firm will not receive the full amount from all of these debtors in the following year.

The calculation of doubtful debts is again recorded as a provision, since the actual bad debts will not be known at this point.

We already know that provision adjustments are normally shown as notes accompanying the trial balance.

- With the provision for doubtful debts:
  - a **new** provision is debited to P&L (treat it as an expense);
  - an **existing** provision is adjusted: any **increase** is debited to P&L;
    any **decrease** is credited to P&L.

For example, if year-end debtors are £45,000, the existing provision (based on last year's debtors) is £200 and this year's provision is to be 5% of year-end debtors, the closing provision will be £225 and therefore the increase of £25 will be debited to P&L.

The finished P&L account will therefore be constructed like this (using the above figures):

	£	£
Gross profit		39,400
Other revenues:		
Commission received		4,320
		43,720
Less expenses:		
Rent	2,800	
Advertising	5,395	
Increase in provision for doubtful debts	25	
Provision for depreciation (vehicles)	14,000	22,220
Net profit		21,500

 Quick check

1. Explain the difference between a prepayment and an accrual.
2. Describe how the accruals and prudence concepts influence accruals, prepayments and provisions in the final accounts.

Section 4   The balance sheet

What are you studying?

This is a statement that we draw up in order to show the firm's financial position. You will study the balance sheet categories, and learn how they display information that helps the users of these statements calculate the firm's profitability and liquidity.

How will you be assessed on this?

Yet again a trial balance is normally given, from which you construct the balance sheet. The typical question requires you to construct trading, profit and loss accounts and the balance sheet, adjusting for given notes, from such a trial balance. When you study the final accounts of partnerships and (in particular) limited companies, the questions in these areas may concentrate to a greater extent on analysing what the balance sheet contains.

Chapter 2 explained the nature of assets and liabilities. These assets and liabilities are normally grouped in the balance sheet under their major headings. These are explained in Table 4.2. Note that we've also included the more complex – but important – summarised definitions given in the ASB's *Statement of Principles for Financial Reporting* (1999).

Working capital

A layout used almost universally, regardless of the type of business organisation, is one where we show the value of the business's **working capital**.

Crucial concept

Working capital is the excess of a firm's current assets over its current liabilities, and is regarded as a good indicator of the firm's liquidity position.

Grouping	Basic definition	ASB definition
Fixed assets	Assets lasting longer than one accounting period, bought not to resell but to help the business make a profit.	Assets are rights or other access to future economic benefits controlled by an entity as a result of past transactions or events.
Current assets	Assets that fluctuate in the short-term, i.e. cash or 'near-cash' items such as stocks and debtors.	
Current liabilities	Short-term debts of the business.	Liabilities are obligations of an entity to transfer economic benefits as a result of past transactions or events.
Long-term liabilities	Amounts owed by the business over more than one accounting period.	
Capital	Investment by the owner(s), affected by profits and drawings.	Ownership interest is the residual amount found by deducting the entity's liabilities from its assets.

Table 4.2 Categories of assets and liabilities

We can calculate the firm's working capital in order to check its ability to meet its short-term debts – this is a commonly examined item.

 Crucial tip — With working capital, you will need to know both **how** and **why** it is calculated. (Study the working capital 'current' ratio on page 157.)

Adjustments affecting the balance sheet

 Crucial tip — The notes accompanying a trial balance normally require **two** adjustments to be made in the final accounts.

The most common adjustments affecting the construction of a sole trader's balance sheet are:

1. Closing stock — Included as a current asset.
2. Depreciation — Fixed assets at cost less **total depreciation to date** (don't just include the single year's depreciation).
3. Doubtful debts — As with depreciation it is closing value of debtors less **year-end total** for doubtful debts (not just the increase/reduction shown in P&L).
4. Accruals — Most accruals are expenses and treated as current liabilities: but check if any represent accrued income, which is a current asset.

5. Prepayments   Again, most are prepaid expenses which are shown as current assets: any prepaid revenue is treated as a current liability.

Layout

The construction and layout of partnership and company accounts are explained later. Here we study a typical layout for a sole trader's balance sheet.

Crucial tip   Be careful with your use of columns: also, study the difference between the two easily confused terms 'net assets' and 'net current assets'.

Balance sheet as at...

	£000	£000	£000
Fixed assets	Cost	Depreciation	Net
Land and buildings	60	15	45
Motor vehicles	20	12	8
	80	27	53
Current assets			
Stock		30	
Debtors and prepayments		23	
Cash and bank		3	
		56	
Current liabilities			
Creditors and accruals		37	
Net current assets			19
Net assets			72
Capital			
Opening balance			52
Net profit			28
			80
Drawings			(8)
			72

Quick check   1. List and describe the main groupings found in the balance sheet.
2. Explain the balance sheet adjustments required for doubtful debts and depreciation.

Section 5 — The final accounts of non-profit-making organisations

What are you studying?   Many organisations in the UK are non-profit-making, such as local clubs and societies. Because they aren't set up to make a profit, they don't draw up orthodox 'profit and loss' accounts, but they still have to keep records of cash movements and of income and expenditure. This Section therefore explains the nature of the various 'club' accounts.

How will you be assessed on this?

The questions on non-profit-making societies tend to be very similar to those set on sole trader final accounts. You may be asked to calculate figures such as the club's cash balance and its accumulated fund (capital), and will probably have to construct the final accounts using the terminology that's relevant to this topic.

The receipts and payments account

Crucial concept

The **receipts and payments** account is another name for a bank account, and therefore records and shows the club's cash position.

What we therefore find in receipts and payments on the receipts (debit) side is cash from subscriptions and from events such as dances (plus associated refreshments); on the payments (cr) side you'll find expense payments and purchases of relevant assets.

Crucial tip

The receipts and payments account (payments side) contains both capital and revenue expenditure, so treat these separately when constructing the final accounts.

Revenue expenditure	**Capital expenditure**
↓	↓
Income and expenditure account	Balance sheet

Another area you're tested on with this account is your knowledge of how the accruals concept works. For example, members' subscriptions received may relate to:

- **this year**: i.e. subscriptions paid this year to cover this year's membership;

- **next year**: i.e. subscriptions received by the club this year **in advance** for next year; and

- **last year**: i.e. subscriptions that were owing at the end of last year which have been paid during this year.

To complicate life, in the subscriptions figure received this year there may be payments due for last year's membership, and there will also probably be unpaid subscriptions owing at the end of this year!

Here's an illustration to show what we do. An amateur dramatic society's record showed this position for its subscriptions, for the year ending 31 December 2002.

1.   Subscriptions received during 2002 totalled £375, of which:
     (a) £15 was for subscriptions relating to 2001;
     (b) £25 was for subscriptions relating to 2003.
2.   Subscriptions received in 2001 relating to 2002 membership year: £40.
3.   Subscriptions still owing at 31 December 2002: £20.

Workings:
Cash received 2002 for 2002 membership = £335 (375 − 15 − 25).
Subscriptions received in 2001 but relevant to 2002: £40.
Subscriptions still owed for 2002: £20 (assuming the prudence concept is not applied).
Total subscriptions income = £395.

Here's the actual subscriptions account (remember, it is a **revenue** account):

Subscriptions account

	£		£
Subscriptions in arrears b/d (owed 2001 for 2002): *dr balance = current asset*	15	Subscriptions in advance b/d (paid in 2001 for 2002): *cr balance = current liability*	40
		Cash received *(the matching dr is in the receipts and payments a/c)*	375
Subscriptions in advance c/d *(paid 2002 for 2003)*	25	Subscriptions in arrears c/d *(still owing at end of 2002)*	20

The difference, i.e. the balance, is (40 + 375 + 20) − (15 + 25) = £395, as we've calculated arithmetically above. This is entered on the debit side of the subscriptions account, with a matching credit entry in the income and expenditure account. The two closing balances are brought down to their 'correct' sides: the subscriptions in advance (cr balance) represents a year-end current liability and the subscriptions in arrears (dr balance) a current asset.

Crucial tip   The organisation may choose to ignore subscriptions in arrears (the prudence concept).

The income and expenditure account

Crucial concept   The purpose of constructing an **income and expenditure account (I&E)** is to calculate whether the organisation has made a surplus or a deficit.

<table>
<tr><td>Crucial concept</td><td>**Surplus** (of income over expenditure) represents the organisation's 'profit': **deficit** (of expenditure over income) represents its 'loss'.</td></tr>
</table>

- In all main respects, the I&E account is the same as a sole trader's P&L account, with subscriptions taking the place of sales.

- Sometimes a separate **trading account** is kept if the organisation runs a profit-making activity (such as a bar) in order to generate profit to support its main activity. In such cases:
  - calculate the profit as normal (income less expenses); and
  - record the profit on the income side of the I&E account.

The balance sheet

This remains a record of the organisation's assets and liabilities at a point in time, and follows the same principles of construction and layout we've already met. **Subscriptions in advance** and **in arrears** often feature in questions and need displaying in the balance sheet.

<table>
<tr><td>Crucial concept</td><td>**Subscriptions in advance** represent prepaid income, and therefore represent a current liability. **Subscriptions in arrears** are owed to the club, and are therefore a potential current asset (though the club may choose to ignore them: prudence concept).</td></tr>
</table>

Using the figures from our earlier illustration, subscriptions in advance at the end of 2002 total £25 (current liability), and subscriptions in arrears are £20 (current asset).

Instead of capital, non-profit-making organisations often use the phrase **accumulated fund** as an alternative.

<table>
<tr><td>Crucial concept</td><td>An organisation's **accumulated fund** acts as its capital: it is the excess of assets over liabilities.</td></tr>
</table>

<table>
<tr><td>Crucial tip</td><td>You are often not given the accumulated fund figure: you can easily calculate it using the accounting equation:

Capital (i.e. accumulated fund) = Assets − Liabilities</td></tr>
</table>

<table>
<tr><td>Quick check</td><td>1. What information does a club's receipts and payments account contain?
2. How are (a) subscriptions in advance, and (b) subscriptions in arrears, treated in a society's balance sheet?
3. How can a club's accumulated fund be calculated if the amount is not stated?</td></tr>
</table>

Section 6   The extended trial balance

What are you studying?

The extended trial balance (ETB) is one way that the various adjustments explained in Sections 2–4 can be 'tracked' and organised. We'll see that its foundation is the traditional trial balance, to which columns are added that show the adjustments made in the final accounts.

How will you be assessed on this?

A popular approach is to give you a part-completed ETB that requires further adjustments to be entered. You then make these adjustments in order to complete the financial statements.

....

You already know the nature and purpose of a trial balance (Chapter 3), and are familiar with the major adjustments that need to be made (pages 75–78).

Crucial concept

The **ETB** is used to display ledger balances and their adjustments, and to calculate the profit figure.

Here is an illustration of how the ETB incorporates the trial balance and adjustments:

Trial balance as at 31 December 2001

	£	£
Bank charges	600	
Rent	7,000	
Power (15 months to 31 March 2002)	2,500	
Business rates	1,500	
Wages and salaries	28,200	
Advertising	1,300	
Sales		144,000
Purchases	92,000	
Machinery (cost)	32,000	
Provision for depreciation: machinery (1.1.2001)		12,500
Vehicles (cost)	18,500	
Provision for depreciation: vehicles (1.1.2001)		9,500
Stocks (1.1.2001)	16,000	
Debtors	43,000	
Provision for doubtful debts (1.1.2001)		2,200
Creditors		28,400
Drawings	17,500	
Capital		63,500
	260,100	260,100

The following adjustments are to be made:

(a) closing stock is valued at £14,000;
(b) depreciation: machinery £4,000; vehicles £3,000;
(c) a debt of £500 is deemed irrecoverable and needs to be written off;
(d) the provision for doubtful debts is to be 5% of year-end debtors;
(e) business rates £200 have been incorrectly classified as advertising;
(f) goods £100 withdrawn for personal use have not been recorded in the accounts;
(g) there is an outstanding rent bill of £1,000 owed at the end of the year.

Step 1: enter the trial balance figures

Our first task is to enter the figures from the trial balance into the relevant ETB columns.

- Task 1: enter these figures into the skeleton structure on page 86.

Step 2: make the adjustments (excluding accruals and prepayments)

We enter the adjustments in the adjustment columns of the ETB.

 Crucial tip

The principle of 'one note = two adjustments' is followed with the ETB, so make sure you study both entries in the adjustment columns.

- Task 2: complete the adjustment columns in the skeleton structure. Use the answer on page 94 to help you if necessary (the workings are explained below).

CLOSING STOCK (A)

This appears in both P&L and balance sheet (BS): in the P&L it reduces the cost of sales (Dr) balance, and is therefore a credit entry; in the BS it is a current asset and therefore a debit balance. Two stock entries are made in the adjustment columns:

Dr Stock (BS)	£14,000	
Cr Stock (P&L)		£14,000

DEPRECIATION (B)

The charges are debited to a depreciation expense a/c – this is added to the list of accounts – and credited to the relevant provision accounts (again, the adjustment columns are used).

Dr Depreciation expense	£7,000	
Cr Provision (machinery)		£4,000
Provision (vehicles)		£3,000

Extended trial balance as at 31 December 2001

Account	Trial balance Dr (£)	Cr (£)	Adjustments Dr (£)	Cr (£)	Profit and loss a/c Dr (£)	Cr (£)	Balance sheet Dr (£)	Cr (£)
Bank charges								
Rent								
Power								
Business rates								
Wages and salaries								
Advertising								
Sales								
Purchases								
Machinery								
Provision for depreciation (machinery)								
Vehicles								
Provision for depreciation (vehicles)								
Stock								
Debtors								
Provision for doubtful debts								
Creditors								
Drawings								
Capital								

BAD DEBT (C) AND PROVISION FOR DOUBTFUL DEBTS (D)

A bad debts expense a/c needs to be created, and is debited with £500; debtors are credited with this amount (i.e. the debtors figure needs reducing). The new provision is 5% of the **adjusted** debtors figure = £2,150 (5% of £43,000). Since the existing provision is £2,200, there is a £50 reduction in the provision. The bad debts expense a/c (created above) is credited with £50 and the provision is debited with £50 through the adjustment columns.

Dr Bad debts expense	£500	
Provision doubtful debts	£50	
Cr Debtors		£500
Bad debts expense		£50

CORRECTING THE ERRORS (E) AND (F)

Business rates a/c must be debited with £500, this amount being credited to advertising. With the 'goods own use' omission, we again use the adjustment columns, this time debiting drawings and crediting purchases with £100.

Dr Business rates	£200	
Cr Advertising		£200
Dr Drawings	£100	
Cr Purchases		£100

Step 3: accruals and prepayments

The trial balance tells us that power has been prepaid for three months at the end of the year. We need to create a prepayments account to record this. Similarly, we set up an accruals account for adjustment (g), rent owing £1,000.

- Task 3: record the appropriate adjustments in the adjustment columns (again, if necessary, check the answer on page 94 to help you).

Dr Prepayments	£500	
Cr Power		£500
Dr Rent	£1,000	
Cr Accruals		£1,000

Step 4: prepare the final accounts

Now that we've recorded all the adjustments in this section of the ETB, the trading, profit and loss accounts and the balance sheet can be prepared. We do this by recording the adjusted (and the non-adjusted) trial balance figures in the appropriate final account column.

Crucial tip — The question to ask here is: is the trial balance item a P&L or a BS item?

- Task 4: transfer the adjusted and non-adjusted balances into the relevant final accounts column. Check your workings with the model answer on page 94.

Step 5: calculating net profit

We need to find the difference between the debit and credit totals in the profit and loss section of the ETB.

Crucial concept — If the credit total is greater, this balance represents net profit: the revenue column is greater than the expense column. If the debit total is the greater, this is a net loss (expenses exceed revenues).

- Task 5: calculate the profit/loss balance and enter it as a balance so the profit and loss column totals agree. Then enter this figure in the balance sheet (profit in the credit column, loss in the debit column) so the balance sheet totals now agree. Check your workings with the model answer on page 94.

Quick check

1. Explain the relationship between the traditional trial balance and the ETB.
2. If the profit and loss columns in the ETB show a debit balance, is this a profit or a loss?

Section 7 — Incomplete records

What are you studying?

There is no guarantee that a business will keep full double-entry records. In practice, a small business may keep little more than a cash book and associated records, from which it can calculate its profit, assets and liabilities.

How will you be assessed on this?

You may be presented with incomplete information and required to draw up final accounts to show profit; the alternative type of question asks you to calculate profit using the accounting equation. Whether or not you're examined directly on this topic, you are likely to be tested in other topic areas on the principles associated with incomplete records.

Page 52 outlined the nature of the accounting equation:

$$\text{Assets} = \text{Capital} + \text{Liabilities}$$

alternatively:

$$\text{Capital} = \text{Assets} - \text{Liabilities}$$

Crucial concept

Profit can be calculated from the increase in the **net worth** of a business, 'net worth' referring to the difference between its assets and its liabilities.

There are two main ways in which the capital figure changes:

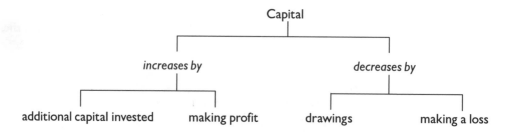

Capital

increases by

additional capital invested   making profit

decreases by

drawings   making a loss

Here are figures for a business. We can use them to demonstrate the steps involved in working out profit from capital changes:

● 1 January, assets total £20,000 and liabilities £4,000;

● 31 December, assets are £22,000 and liabilities £5,500;

● during the year drawings are £3,500, and £1,000 more capital has been invested.

1. Calculate opening capital. $C = A - L = 20,000 - 4,000 = 16,000$.
2. Calculate closing capital. $C = A - L = 22,000 - 5,500 = 16,500$.

The £500 increase in capital would represent profit if drawings have not been made and/or any additional capital has not been invested.

3. Adjust for drawings and any capital invested:

	£
Capital increase	500
Add back drawings	3,500
	4,000
Less new capital invested	(1,000)
Profit for the year	**3,000**

The second type of question requiring you to construct final accounts tests two important principles:

● (opening) capital may not be given – we can calculate it using the accounting equation, i.e. assets minus liabilities;

● expense and revenue figures may have to be calculated using the accruals concept, e.g. where a cash figure has to be adjusted using the same principles we studied for a club's subscriptions figure (page 81)

 Crucial tip   Remember to apply the principle: does it refer to this year? If 'yes', include it; if 'no', exclude it.

To reinforce the second point above, here are two illustrations. First, let's assume:

● £500 has been paid for stationery during the year;

● the opening stock of stationery was £45;

● the closing stock is £25.

The figure for the cost of stationery will be:

$$£500 \quad \text{paid}$$
$$+ £45 \quad \text{stock at start (used this year)}$$
$$- £25 \quad \text{stock at close (bought this year but}$$
$$\text{to be used next year)}$$
$$= \textbf{£520}$$

Second, we may be given opening and/or closing figures for prepayments or accruals. For example:

● power bill owing at start of year £58;

● £690 paid for power during the year;

● £12 prepaid for power at the end of the year.

The cost of power is therefore £690 paid − £58 accrued (paid this year but applying to last year) − £12 prepaid (again paid this year, but applying to next year).

1. Explain whether an increase in capital represents an increase in profit.
2. What principle do we apply to calculate expenses/revenues from given cash figures?

Crucial examples

1. Identify the relevant concept that each of the following illustrates:

   (a) creating a provision for doubtful debts;
   (b) the capital account is used to record the owner's investment;
   (c) valuing machines at their cost, rather than their resale, value;
   (d) a debit and credit entry is made;
   (e) showing a bill owing at the end of a period as a liability for that period;
   (f) continuing to use the same method of depreciation for the same type of fixed assets.

2. Simon Travis's trial balance at 30 June 2002 was:

	£	£
Capital		166,300
Drawings	18,400	
Purchases and sales	36,180	100,400
Purchases returns and sales returns	800	280
Discounts allowed and received	910	700
Stock (1 July 2001)	8,100	
Salaries	29,100	
Rates and insurance	5,230	
Marketing and advertising	3,060	
Loan from finance company		10,000
Debtors and creditors	17,400	16,120
Cash at bank	5,020	
Land and buildings	91,500	
Machinery at cost	75,000	
Provision for depreciation (machinery)		15,000
Vehicles at cost	38,100	
Provision for depreciation (vehicles)		20,000
	328,800	328,800

Notes at 30 June 2002:

(a) stock £8,400;
(b) rates prepaid £350;
(c) advertising bill owing £150;
(d) the debtors figure includes £600 which is not expected to be recovered;
(e) loan interest is charged at 10% on the loan balance: no entries have been made;
(f) depreciation is to be charged: machinery £7,500; vehicles £10,000;
(g) included in salaries is £750 paid to employees when repairing the roof of Simon Travis's house.

Prepare the final accounts for Simon Travis.

3. The assets and liabilities of the Viola Club on 1 April 2001 were: premises £30,000; furniture £12,000; bar stocks £150; and bank balance £600.

The club's receipts and payments account details are:

	£		£
Balance	600	Bar supplies	4,300
Subscriptions	480	Raffle prizes	60
Bar sales	4,750	Annual dance expenses	130
Raffle ticket sales	150	Cost of refreshments	80
Annual dance receipts	200	Rates	250
Sale of refreshments	160	Electricity	500
		Repairs to equipment	200
		New equipment	200
		Closing balance	620
	6,340		6,340

On 31 March 2002, bar stocks were £200, £80 was owing for electricity and rates were prepaid by £45.

Prepare the club's financial statements.

4. The balances from a business's records were as follows (31 December):

	2000 (£)	2001 (£)
Fixed assets	18,850	18,850
Stocks	2,861	3,246
Debtors	1,534	1,262
Bank	621	1,938
Creditors	2,118	2,202

The owner withdrew £12,400 from the business for private use, and paid another £2,400 additional capital into the business. The owner depreciates fixed assets by 20% each year.

Calculate the owner's profit for 2001.

5. Explain each of these terms:

Accounting concepts	Net profit
Accumulated fund	Net worth
Carriage	Provision
Deficit	Receipts and payments a/c
Depreciation	Reducing balance method
Doubtful debts	Straight line
Drawings	Subscriptions
ETB	Surplus
Gross profit	Working capital
Income and expenditure a/c	

Answers

1. (a) prudence
   (b) entity
   (c) going concern
   (d) duality
   (e) accruals
   (f) consistency.

2. **Simon Travis**:

   Trading, profit and loss accounts for year ending 30 June 2002

	£	£
Sales		100,400
Less sales returns		(800)
		99,600
Less cost of sales:		
Opening stock	8,100	
Purchases (36,180 − 280)	35,900	
Closing stock	(8,400)	35,600
Gross profit		64,000
Discount received		700
		64,700
Less expenses:		
Discount allowed	910	
Salaries (29,100 − 750)	28,350	
Rates and insurance (5,230 − 350)	4,880	
Marketing and advertising (3,060 +150)	3,210	
Loan interest	1,000	
Bad debts	600	
Depreciation (machinery)	7,500	
Depreciation (vehicles)	10,000	56,450
Net profit		8,250

   Simon Travis: Balance sheet as at 30 June 2002

	£	£	£
Fixed assets:			
Land and buildings	91,500	–	91,500
Machinery	75,000	22,500	52,500
Vehicles	38,100	30,000	8,100
	204,600	52,500	152,100
Current assets:			
Stock		8,400	
Debtors (17,400 − 600)		16,800	
Prepayments		350	
Bank		5,020	
		30,570	

   ..../

	£	£	£
Current liabilities:			
Creditors	16,120		
Accruals (150 + 1000)	1,150	17,270	
Net current assets			13,300
			165,400
Long-term liabilities:			
Loan			(10,000)
Net assets			155,400
Capital:			
Opening balance			166,300
Net profit			8,250
			174,550
Drawings (18,400 + 750)			(19,150)
			155,400

3. Viola Club: income and expenditure account, year ending 31 March 2002:

Expenditure:	£	Income:	£
Rates (250 − 45)	205	Bar profit	500 *
Electricity (500 + 80)	580	Raffle net income (150 − 60)	90
Repairs to equipment**	200	Dance net income (200 − 130)	70
Surplus	235	Refreshment net income (160 − 80)	80
		Subscriptions	480
	1,220		1,220

*Bar trading account: opening stock £150 + purchases £4,300 − closing stock £200 = cost of sales £4,250; deduct from sales £4,750 = £500 profit.

** Note the new equipment is omitted (capital expenditure).

Viola Club: balance sheet as at 31 March 2002 (opening accumulated fund = £42,750, i.e. the four opening assets added together):

Assets:	£	Liabilities:	£
Premises	30,000	Accumulated fund	42,750
Furniture (12,000 + 200)	12,200	Surplus	235
Stocks	200	Accrued expense	80
Prepaid expense	45		
Bank	620		
	43,065		43,065

4. Capital figures (assets less liabilities): £21,748 in 2000, and £19,324 in 2001 (the fixed assets are valued at £15,080).

	£
Closing capital	19,324
Add back drawings	12,400
Less capital invested	(2,400)
Less opening capital	(21,748)
Profit	**7,576**

5. Check your answers against the **Crucial concepts** in the chapter.

Model answer to Section 6: Extended trial balance as at 31 December 2001

Account	Trial Balance Dr (£)	Cr (£)	Adjustments Dr (£)	Cr (£)	Profit and loss a/c Dr (£)	Cr (£)	Balance sheet Dr (£)	Cr (£)
Bank charges	600				600			
Rent	7,000		1,000		8,000			
Power	2,500			500	2,000			
Business rates	1,500		200		1,700			
Wages and salaries	28,200				28,200			
Advertising	1,300			200	1,100			
Sales		144,000				144,000		
Purchases	92,000			100	91,900			
Machinery	32,000						32,000	
Provision for depreciation (machinery)		12,500		4,000				16,500
Vehicles	18,500						18,500	
Provision for depreciation (vehicles)		9,500		3,000				12,500
Stock	16,000		14,000	14,000	16,000	14,000	14,000	
Debtors	43,000			500			42,500	
Provision for doubtful debts		2,200	50					2,150
Creditors		28,400						28,400
Drawings	17,500		100				17,600	
Capital		63,500						63,500
Depreciation expense			7,000		7,000			
Bad debts expense			500	50	450			
Prepayments			500				500	
Accruals				1,000				1,000
Subtotals (profit and loss columns)					156,950	158,000		
Net profit					1,050			1,050
Totals	260,100	260,100	23,350	23,350	158,000	158,000	125,100	125,100

Crucial reading and research

Reading

These books provide more information on basic final accounts.

Dodge, R. (1997) *Foundations of Business Accounting*, 2nd edn. International Thomson Business Press (ISBN 1 86512 153 7). See Chapter 6, 'End of period adjustments'.

Dyson, J. R. (1994) *Accounting for Non-Accounting Students*. 3rd edn. Pitman Publishing (ISBN 0 273 60435 X). See Chapter 4, 'Basic financial statements'.

Glautier, M. W. E. and Underdown, B. (1997) *Accounting Theory and Practice*, 6th edn. Pitman Publishing (ISBN 0 273 62444 X). See Chapter 9, 'Double-entry bookkeeping and periodic measurement', accruals and prepayments, stock adjustments; Chapter 10, 'Losses in asset values and periodic measurement', depreciation, doubtful debts; Chapter 11, 'Preparing a profit and loss account and a balance sheet'.

Research

The ASB's *Statement of Principles for Financial Reporting* (1999) – see Chapter 6 – identifies and defines the elements of financial statements in its Chapter 4. It is well worth researching into these definitions and meanings – particularly those for **gains** and **losses –** and this research will help you assess how an accounting item is classified (e.g. as either an asset or a liability).

It is also worthwhile studying the published accounts of PLCs. As financial statements, they are much more complex than the statements illustrated in this Chapter, but it's a valuable exercise for you to explore how the basic structures explained here are still relevant to published accounts.

Do you or your friends have links with any clubs or societies? If so, perhaps you could arrange to research into how they keep their financial records.

PARTNERSHIP ACCOUNTS

Chapter summary

This Chapter covers the nature and accounting requirements of partnerships. Because they are unlimited liability organisations without a separate legal existence, partnerships are similar to sole traders. There are some important differences in how the personal and final accounts of a partnership are constructed, so this Chapter explains appropriation of profits, the construction of partners' personal accounts and what happens in the event of a change in the partnership.

Studying this Chapter will help you to:

- appropriate profit between two or more partners;
- distinguish between capital and current accounts;
- account for changes in the partnership;
- carry out the entries required to dissolve a partnership; and
- understand and use appropriately the various terms that you will meet when undertaking partnership accounts.

Assessment targets

Target 1: explaining the nature of appropriation

In your assessment, you will be given a profit figure and may be asked to explain how it is normally appropriated. Exercise 1 at the end of the Chapter assesses your ability to do this.

Target 2: carrying out the appropriation of profit

You will be required to distribute profit between the various partners, using an appropriation and personal accounts. Exercise 2 at the end of the Chapter tests you on this.

Target 3: understanding, and accounting for, goodwill

You will have to define and account for the intangible asset of goodwill. Exercise 3 at the end of the Chapter links goodwill to capital accounts, and tests your knowledge of the appropriate procedures.

Target 4: accounting for partners leaving or joining the partnership

You may be asked to close a partnership's books. Exercise 4 at the end of the Chapter assesses your understanding of this, and of a particular procedure we apply when a partner is insolvent.

Target 5: using accounting terms appropriately

Throughout your assessments, you will have to use partnership terms appropriately. Exercise 5 at the end of the Chapter tests you on these terms.

Crucial concepts

These are the key terms and concepts you will meet in this Chapter:

Appropriation account	Interest on capital
Balance of profits	Interest on drawings
Current account	Partnership salary
Garner v *Murray*	Realisation account
Goodwill	Revaluation account

Relevant links

Chapter 4 has shown you how to construct basic final accounts. When you study Chapter 6, you'll be able to compare the final accounts of a partnership with those of a limited company.

Section I — Partnership basics

What are you studying?

This Section sets the scene for partnership accounts. Here we outline the background to accounting for partnerships, notably how the partners agree to share the firm's net profit, and the law associated with this. To understand the content of this Chapter, make sure you're familiar with how (sole trader) final accounts are constructed (Chapter 4).

How will you be assessed on this?

You will need this background knowledge in order to answer detailed questions on partnership accounts. It is possible that you will be tested on your understanding of the 1890 Partnership Act, but it is more likely that the examiner will get you to apply these general principles when calculating the partners' share of net profits.

Partners are free to make whatever agreement they wish concerning how they share net profit. The **partnership agreement** contains details on partners' capital and drawings, and also states how profit is to be **appropriated,** normally using three main headings.

I. Interest on capital

This method used to share partnership profits is based on the idea that the partner who invests more in the business, i.e. **risks** more (remember unlimited liability normally applies here), should receive a larger share of the profits. If you're also studying economics, this is an example of opportunity cost: since partners can't invest this capital in, say, a building society, they are losing the interest they would otherwise have earned from this type of investment.

Crucial concept — **Interest on capital** is a way to appropriate some of the net profit, and is based on the fact that partners tend to invest unequal amounts in the business.

Crucial tip — Don't confuse 'interest' in this context with the interest actually paid on investments.

2. Partners' salaries

This is the way in which a partnership may reward partners who invest more time (perhaps in lieu of investing more money) in the partnership. Like interest on capital, it is a way of appropriating profit – in this case, of rewarding the partner doing the most work.

> **Crucial concept** **Partnership salary** is the way in which some of the net profit can be appropriated to reward the partner investing more of his/her time in the partnership.

3. Residue of profits

Salary and interest on capital are deducted from the net profit: the remaining balance is shared between the partners.

> **Crucial concept** **Residue (balance) of profits** occurs after deduction of salaries and interest on capitals. This balance is shared according to the partners' agreed profit-sharing ratios.

Interest on drawings

Sometimes partners arrange to charge interest on drawings. This penalty may dissuade them from withdrawing more cash (or goods) than absolutely necessary, because the more cash that is withdrawn, the greater the adverse effect on the partnership's liquidity.

> **Crucial concept** **Interest on drawings** is charged to discourage partners from withdrawing excessive amounts of cash out of the partnership.

The 1890 Partnership Act

You may be asked to explain the position where there is no partnership agreement. This Act states that:

- residual profits and losses are to be shared equally;
- there is no entitlement to interest on capitals (and no interest on drawings);
- there is also no entitlement to a partnership salary;
- any loan made by the partners over and above their capitals will receive interest at 5% per annum.

> **Crucial tip** Don't forget that this Act only applies where there is **no agreement** to the contrary.

 Quick check

1. Explain why partners may use (a) interest on capital, and (b) salaries, as methods of appropriating their profits.
2. State the main provisions of the Partnership Act 1890. Under what circumstances will this Act apply to a partnership?

Section 2 · The appropriation account and the current accounts

What are you studying?

In this Section we explore the fundamental accounting problem of partnership final accounts: how to split one profit between more than one partner. We've just studied the ways in which profit can be appropriated. Here, we explain how the appropriation account actually works, and how individual partners' profits are recorded in their personal accounts.

How will you be assessed on this?

Many partnership questions actually start by giving you a net profit figure, and then ask you to appropriate it according to the partnership agreement. These questions tend to be based on an existing partnership that is not changing (i.e., no new or departing partners). You show your understanding of the book-keeping entries involved by constructing the appropriation account and the partners' current accounts.

Crucial concept

The **appropriation account** records partnership appropriations of profit.

In the appropriation account we start with the net profit figure.

Crucial tip

You may be asked to adjust the NP figure, e.g. where a P&L expense such as loan interest has been omitted.

Debit (i.e. deduct)		Credit (i.e. add)
Interest on capital	In all cases, the	Interest on
Salary	matching entry is made	drawings
Share (residue) of profit	in the current a/cs	

Here's an illustration. Two partners, A and B, share profits and losses in the ratio 1 : 2. They agree that A receives a partnership salary of £7,000, and interest on their capitals is at 10%. Their account balances are:

Capital a/cs	A £20,000	Current a/cs	A £4,000 (cr)
	B £80,000		B £2,000 (dr)

During the year, drawings made were: A £6,000 and B £4,000. Interest is charged on these drawings at 10%. Net profit for the year totalled £49,000.

Here is the appropriation account for A and B:

Appropriation account		£	£
Net profit b/d (from P&L)			49,000
Interest on drawings:	Partner A		600
	Partner B		400
			50,000
Interest on capitals:	A	2,000	
	B	8,000	(10,000)
Partnership salary:	A		(7,000)
			33,000
Share of profits:	A (⅓)		(11,000)
	B (⅔)		(22,000)

 Crucial tip　Students often either forget to include interest on drawings, or they subtract it from, instead of adding it to, net profit.

The capital and current accounts

Unlike a sole trader's capital account, which records capital, profit and drawings, the partners normally use **current accounts** to keep profit and drawings separate from capital. We can show this diagramatically, by 'cutting' the sole trader's capital account in two:

Sole trader capital account　=　Partner's capital and current accounts

	Capital balance
Less drawings	Add profit

The partner's capital a/c

	Capital balance
Less drawings	Add profit

The partner's current a/c

To construct a partner's current account, remember the above summary, which shows us:

Any current account

Drawings	**Profit**
side	side

You will also be given a current account opening balance. Sometimes the question doesn't state whether it is a credit or debit balance: in such cases, we assume it is a **credit** balance.

	Current account debit balance	Current account credit balance
	Overdrawn profit	**Undrawn** profit
	Balance sheet **asset**	Balance sheet **liability**
	(Partner owes firm the balance)	(Firm owes Partner the balance)

Crucial concept   A partner's **current account** records the individual partner's share of profits, and any drawings made. A partner's **capital account** shows the individual partner's capital balance.

Using the figures from our above example (the matching double-entry with the appropriation account is shown in italics):

Current accounts

	A	B		A	B
	£	£		£	£
Opening balance		2,000	Opening balance	4,000	
Drawings	6,000	4,000	*Interest on capitals*	*2,000*	*8,000*
Interest on drawings	*600*	*400*	*Salary*	*7,000*	
(Closing balance	17,400	23,600)	*Share of profits*	*11,000*	*22,000*

Crucial tip   Forgetting to include the drawings figure in the current account is another common error.

Figure 5.1 shows us the relationship between the various partnership ledger and final accounts:

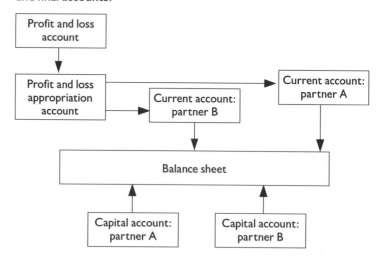

Figure 5.1 Relationship between ledger and final accounts for a partnerhsip

Section 3 — Changes in the partnership

What are you studying?

We already know (from page 23) that, unlike limited companies, a change in the ownership of a partnership affects the continuity of the business. Any new partner entering the business, or old partner leaving it, causes a new partnership to be created. The accounts of the partnership must reflect these changes, and so here we study the relevant adjustments we must make to the partners' capital and current accounts.

How will you be assessed on this?

Questions involving the introduction of a new partner, or the death or retirement of an existing one, give you the 'old' and 'new' positions of the partnership. With these questions, you will be expected to adjust the partners' capital accounts as a result of the changes.

You may also be asked to revalue certain partnership assets or liabilities, and to account for this revaluation. Again, these questions test your knowledge of how the partners' capital and current accounts function.

....

Although the legal position is that any change in the partners requires a new partnership to be set up, we adopt a simpler approach from the accounting point of view: we make **adjustments** to the partners' personal accounts. The nature of these adjustments varies, depending on the type of change to the partnership.

 Crucial tip — Unlike appropriation of profits, we use the partners' capital accounts to record the main adjustments as a result of changes in the partnership.

When an existing partner retires or dies

- We calculate the leaving partner's **share of the partnership assets** in order to transfer this value to her/him (or the personal representative).

- As a result of applying the going concern and historical cost concepts, the true worth of the partnership at the time of leaving will normally exceed its book value (assets − liabilities): a revaluation often takes place so the leaving partner receives a fair share of the business net worth.

- A **revaluation account** is used to obtain the total **profit/loss on revaluation**.

- Profits/losses on revaluation are entered in the partners' capital accounts in the **agreed profit-sharing ratio**.

A **revaluation** account calculates the profit or loss on revaluation as a result of a change in the partnership.

As an example, let's assume that Scary, Baby and Ginger are in partnership, but Ginger decides to leave the partnership. At the time of leaving, the partners shared profits in the ratio Scary ³⁄₁₀, Baby ⁵⁄₁₀, Ginger ²⁄₁₀. The following assets were revalued:

	Book value £	Revaluation £
Property	120,000	150,000
Equipment (net)	35,000	27,000
Debtors	15,500	13,500

You may be expected to use the journal to show these revaluations:

	£	£
Property	30,000	
Revaluation account		30,000
Being profit on revaluation		

	£	£
Revaluation account	10,000	
Equipment		8,000
Debtors		2,000
Being losses on revaluation.		

You can see from the journal that the revaluation account has a net credit balance of £20,000. This represents an overall profit on revaluation (a credit balance), and will be transferred to – shared between – the partners using their profit-sharing ratios. The journal entry will be:

	£	£
Revaluation account	20,000	
Scary capital account		6,000
Baby capital account		10,000
Ginger capital account		4,000
Being profit on revaluation divided between partners.		

Crucial tip

There is no guarantee of a profit on revaluation, so be prepared to debit any loss on revaluation to the partners' capital accounts.

Goodwill

One of the most common adjustments in the partnership books involves establishing the value of goodwill. The phrase 'the whole is greater than the sum of its parts' summarises goodwill nicely: it arises as a result of factors such as good management and staff, good location, good quality product, the firm's reputation, and so on.

Goodwill is an intangible fixed asset: it is the excess of the price paid for a business as a going concern over its 'net worth' (the value of the individual assets less liabilities).

Any partner leaving the partnership will be entitled to the share of the goodwill she/he has helped create. If we assume our partners calculate their firm's goodwill to be £40,000 at the time Ginger leaves, the adjustment is:

	£	£
Goodwill	40,000	
Scary capital (³/₁₀)		12,000
Baby capital (⁵/₁₀)		20,000
Ginger capital (²/₁₀)		8,000

Ginger has therefore received a total of £12,000 as a result of revaluing assets and valuing goodwill.

The remaining partners have two questions to answer:

- What is our new profit-sharing relationship? (We'll assume a new profit-sharing arrangement of Scary ²/₅ and Baby ³/₅)

- Do we keep goodwill in the accounts?

If the partners keep a goodwill account, no further entries are required. If, however, they decide to eliminate goodwill, the remaining partners do this using the **new profit-sharing ratios**:

	£	£
Scary capital (²/₅)	16,000	
Baby capital (³/₅)	24,000	
Goodwill		40,000
Being goodwill written off.		

The main reason goodwill often doesn't feature in the books is that it is an **intangible** asset: the prudence concept suggests it should be eliminated from the books.

When a new partner joins the partnership

Any new partner who joins a successful firm will benefit from the existence of goodwill (whether recorded in the books or not). Conversely, the existing partners now have to share this benefit with an additional partner who – as a new partner – has made no contribution to the success of the firm, and thus no contribution to the creation of the goodwill. As a result, we have to compensate the existing partners for this loss of goodwill due to the incoming partner.

- The new partner will bring new **capital** into the firm, and so the new partner's capital account will be credited with this amount.

- Any gains (or losses) from revaluation are divided between the **existing partners** using their old profit-sharing ratio.

- Goodwill is dealt with as follows:
  If a goodwill account is **not** opened;

  - credit the existing (old) partners' capital accounts with their share of goodwill using the existing profit-sharing ratio;
  - debit the new partners (again, using the capital account) with their share of goodwill using the new profit-sharing ratio.

  If a goodwill account **is** opened, it is debited and the existing partners' capital accounts are credited (using the existing profit-sharing ratio) with the value of goodwill.

Crucial tip   This goodwill adjustment compensates the existing partners for their reduced share of goodwill as a result of the new partner joining.

Quick check

1. Explain why the partners often decide to revalue assets and liabilities when there is a change in the partnership.

2. How does goodwill affect partnership accounts when there is a change in the partnership?

Section 4	**Partnership dissolution**

What are you studying?

Partners may decide to dissolve (finish) their partnership. In such cases, the partnership ceases to exist. We must therefore study the book-keeping entries required to dissolve a partnership.

How will you be assessed on this?

Questions to do with dissolving a partnership will give you details of the partnership's balance sheet at the time of dissolution. You then have to follow a set procedure to realise the assets (i.e. turn them into cash), pay off the liabilities and transfer the remaining cash balances to each partner.

We'll use an example to study the steps involved in dissolution.

Rag, Tag and Bobtail, who share profits equally, decided to dissolve their partnership on 1 January 2002. The firm's balance sheet at this date was:

		£000			£000	£000
Capitals:	Rag	22	Fixed assets (net):			
	Tag	22	Furniture			35
	Bobtail	10	Vehicles			25
Current accounts:						60
	Rag	8	Current assets:			
	Tag	(2)	Stock		8	
	Bobtail	6	Debtors		9	
			Bank		4	
Bank loan		12	Current liabilities:			
			Creditors		(3)	18
		78				78

The bank loan was repaid; furniture was sold for £32,000; Tag took over a company car (book value £7,000) for £8,000, and the other vehicles were sold for £19,000. Debtors realised £8,000, and the firm gained from creditors' discounts, paying off creditors for £2,000. Stock was sold for £5,000. Dissolution expenses totalled £2,000.

Step 1: combine the partners' capital and current accounts

Partners' accounts

	Rag £000	Tag £000	Bobtail £000		Rag £000	Tag £000	Bobtail £000
				Capitals	22	22	10
Current a/c		2		Current accounts	8		6

Step 2: open a realisation account, and transfer assets and liabilities (except cash) at book values

Realisation account

	£000		£000
Furniture	35	Bank loan	12
Vehicles	25	Creditors	3
Stock	8		
Debtors	9		

Bank account

	£000	
Balance	4	

Crucial concept   A **realisation account** is used to calculate any profit or loss when ending the partnership.

Crucial tip   We now have only three accounts opened: partners, realisation and bank.

Step 3: record the double-entry sale of assets and payment of liabilities using the realisation and bank accounts

Crucial tip   Record any partners' retention of assets in the partner's account, not the bank account.

Step 4: record the expenses of realisation in the realisation (dr) and bank (cr) accounts

Realisation account

	£000		£000
Furniture	35	Bank loan	12
Vehicles	25	Creditors	3
Stock	8	Furniture	32
Debtors	9	Tag (car)	8
Bank loan	12	Vehicles	19
Creditors	2	Debtors	8
Expenses	2	Stock	5

Bank account

	£000		£000
Balance	4	Loan	12
Furniture	32	Creditors	2
Vehicles	19	Expenses	2
Debtors	8		
Stock	5		

Partners' accounts

	Rag £000	Tag £000	Bobtail £000		Rag £000	Tag £000	Bobtail £000
				Capitals	22	22	10
Current accounts		2		Current accounts	8		6
Vehicle		8					

Step 5: transfer the balance on realisation to the partners, using their profit-sharing ratio

Crucial tip   A credit balance on realisation = profit; a debit balance = loss.

The balance in this example is £6,000 (dr), representing a loss. The partners share this equally.

Step 6: transfer the cash to the partners
Calculate for each partner the balance on the account, and transfer the relevant amount from the bank account.

Crucial tip · The balance on the cash (bank) account must equal the total of the partners' balances (if not, an error has been made).

Realisation account					Bank account				
	£000		£000			£000		£000
Furniture	35	Bank loan	12		Balance	4	Loan	12
Vehicles	25	Creditors	3		Furniture	32	Creditors	2
Stock	8	Furniture	32		Vehicles	19	Expenses	2
Debtors	9	Tag (car)	8		Debtors	8	**Rag**	28
Bank loan	12	Vehicles	19		Stock	5	**Tag**	10
Creditors	2	Debtors	8			—	**Bobtail**	14
Expenses	2	Stock	5			68		68
		Loss: Rag	2					
		Loss: Tag	2					
		Loss: Bobtail	2					
	93		93					

Partners' accounts

	Rag	Tag	Bobtail			Rag	Tag	Bobtail
	£000	£000	£000			£000	£000	£000
					Capitals	22	22	10
Current account		2			Current accounts	8		6
Vehicle		8						
Share of loss	2	2	2					
Bank	28	10	14					
	30	22	16			30	22	16

Insolvency

We've illustrated how partners share profits and losses on realisation in normal circumstances. We may find, however, that at the end of realisation one of the partners is in deficit to the firm. If the partner is **insolvent** and cannot make good this loss, the **rule in *Garner* v *Murray*** (1904) is applied.

Crucial concept · The rule in *Garner* v *Murray* states that, in the event of a partner being insolvent, losses are shared in the ratio of the last agreed capital balances.

Crucial tip · Many partnership agreements deliberately exclude this rule, stating that the partners bear the loss in their profit-sharing ratio.

Quick check

1. List the steps involved in realisation.
2. When does the rule in *Garner* v *Murray* come into operation?

Crucial examples

1. (a) What is the purpose of an appropriation account?
    (b) Name **four** items that will be found in both an appropriation and a current account.

2. Arthur and Brian are in partnership, and for the year ending 31.12.2002 their firm made a profit of £125,000. Their agreement is that:

    (a) Each receives interest at 5% on the balance of their capital accounts.
    (b) A salary of £5,000 per annum is paid to Arthur, and £15,000 to Brian.
    (c) During the year Arthur withdrew £24,000 and Brian £31,000. Interest is to be charged: Arthur £1,200, Brian £1,550.
    (d) Any residue of profits is shared: Arthur ⅗, Brian ⅖.

    At 1 January 2002 the balances in the firm's books were:

	Arthur	Brian
	£	£
Capital accounts:	50,000	25,000
Current accounts (cr):	12,400	8,600

    Prepare the appropriation and current accounts.

3. Sand and Gravel are equal partners in a building firm run as a partnership. Their capitals are: Sand £24,000, Gravel £18,000. Cement is to join as a new partner on 1 January 2002, and will invest £8,000 as capital and £5,000 as his share of the goodwill. The new agreement is that the partners will share profits in the ratio of Sand ⅖, Gravel ⅖ and Cement ⅕, and that a goodwill account will not be opened in the partnership books.

    Prepare the partners' capital accounts.

4. Leo, Dee and Caprio were partners, sharing profits 3:2:1. After completing their realisation account, their personal accounts are as follows:

Personal accounts

	Leo	Dee	Caprio		Leo	Dee	Caprio
	£	£	£		£	£	£
Realisation account:				Capitals	20,000	10,000	10,000
Losses	21,000	14,000	7,000	Current a/cs	3,500	1,000	1,000
Balances c/d	2,500		4,000	Balance c/d		3,000	
	23,500	14,000	11,000		23,500	14,000	11,000
Balance b/d		3,000		Balances b/d	2,500		4,000

Explain the position if:
(a) Dee is able to meet the debt owed;
(b) Dee is declared insolvent and cannot pay the amount owed.

5. Explain each of these terms:

Appropriation account	Interest on capital
Balance of profits	Interest on drawings
Current account	Partnership salary
Garner v Murray	Realisation account
Goodwill	Revaluation account

Answers

1. (a) To share the net profit between the partners.
   (b) Interest on drawings; interest on capital; partnership salary; share (residue) of profits.

2.

Arthur and Brian

Appropriation account for year ending 31 December 2002

		£	£	£
Net profit b/d				125,000
Interest on drawings:	Arthur		1,200	
	Brian		1,550	2,750
				127,750
Interest on capitals:	Arthur	2,500		
	Brian	1,250		(3,750)
Partnership salary:	Arthur	5,000		
	Brian	15,000		(20,000)
				104,000
Share of profits:	Arthur (⅗)			(62,400)
	Brian (⅖)			(41,600)

Current accounts

	Arthur	Brian		Arthur	Brian
	£	£		£	£
Drawings	24,000	31,000	Opening balances	12,400	8,600
Interest on drawings	1,200	1,550	Interest on capitals	2,500	1,250
			Salaries	5,000	15,000
Closing balances	57,100	33,900	Share of profits	62,400	41,600
	82,300	66,450		82,300	66,450

3.

Capital accounts

	Sand	Gravel	Cement		Sand	Gravel	Cement
	£	£	£		£	£	£
Goodwill (new):				Balances b/d	24,000	18,000	
Sand (⅖)	10,000			Capital introduced			8,000
Gravel (⅖)		10,000		Goodwill (existing):			
Cement (⅕)			5,000	Sand (½)	12,500		
Balances c/d	26,500	20,500	3,000	Gravel (½)		12,500	
	36,500	30,500	8,000		36,500	30,500	8,000

(Goodwill is valued at £25,000 because Cement introduced **£5,000** as his **one-fifth share**.)

4. (a) The bank balance will be £3,500 (2,500 + 4,000 – 3,000). Dee will pay £3,000 into the bank, boosting its balance to £6,500. Leo and Caprio can now receive the money each is owed: £2,500 and £4,000 respectively.

(b) Since Dee cannot pay any money, the loss of Dee's £3,000 is borne by Leo and Caprio in the ratio of their last agreed capital balances: the *Garner v Murray* rule. Leo bears £2,000 and Caprio £1,000. (It is **not** shared 3:1 due to Dee's insolvency.)

The partners' accounts will be closed as follows:

Personal accounts

	Leo £	Dee £	Caprio £		Leo £	Dee £	Caprio £
Realisation account:				Capitals	20,000	10,000	10,000
Losses	21,000	14,000	7,000	Current a/cs	3,500	1,000	1,000
Balances c/d	2,500		4,000	Balance c/d		3,000	
	23,500	14,000	11,000		23,500	14,000	11,000
Balance b/d		3,000		Balances b/d	2,500		4,000
Dee's deficit	2,000		1,000	Leo and Caprio		3,000	
Bank	500		3,000				

(The £500 + £3,000 paid to Leo and Caprio equals the £3,500 available in the bank.)

5. Check your answers against the **Crucial Concepts** in the Chapter.

Crucial research and reading

Reading

These books provide more information on partnership accounts:

Dodge, R. (1997) *Foundations of Business Accounting*, 2nd edn. International Thomson Business Press (ISBN 1 86512 153 7). See Chapter 14, 'Partnerships: introduction', and Chapter 15, 'Partnerships: changes in ownership'.

Wood, F. and Sangster, A. (1999) *Business Accounting*, 8th edn. Financial Times/Pitman Publishing (ISBN 0 273 63742 8). See Chapter 42, 'Partnership accounts: an introduction', Chapter 43, 'Goodwill for sole traders and partnerships', Chapter 44, 'Revaluation of partnership assets' and Chapter 45, 'Partnership dissolution'.

Research

On 20 July 2000 the **Limited Liability Partnerships Act** received royal assent. The essential feature of a limited liability partnership (LLP) is that it offers limited liability to its members while retaining the flexibility and tax status of a partnership.

Although the LLP is unlikely to dominate the UK economy, it is such a rare event to have a new form of business organisation created. You will find research into LLPs interesting and informative. One source (check under Acts, 2000) is:

- www.legislation.hmso.gov.uk/

CHAPTER 6

LIMITED COMPANY
ACCOUNTS

Chapter summary

This Chapter contains information about limited company final accounts. These financial statements are drawn up by companies, and act as records of their financial position and performance. In constructing these accounts, there are certain rules regarding content and layout that must be followed.

Studying this Chapter will help you to:

- describe and differentiate between the main types of share and loan capital;

- construct a limited company profit loss account, using a suitable layout;

- construct a balance sheet, using the normal headings found in company accounts;

- outline and explain the nature of the major FRSs and SSAPs that influence the final accounts of companies; and

- understand and use appropriately the various names and terms you'll meet when studying and constructing these final accounts.

Assessment targets

Target 1: understanding share and loan capital

In your assessment, you will be required to enter and use figures for share and loan capital appropriately. Exercise 1 at the end of the Chapter assesses your ability to do this.

Target 2: constructing final accounts

You will have to use figures, normally from a trial balance, in creating final accounts for a company. Exercises 2 and 3 at the end of the Chapter test you on this.

Target 3: understanding and using FRS and SSAP informaton

It's valuable to know the key company account 'rules' when studying these accounts. Exercise 4 at the end of the Chapter tests your understanding of these rules.

Target 4: using accounting terms appropriately

Throughout your assessments, you will have to use company-related accounting terms appropriately. Exercise 5 at the end of the Chapter assesses whether you can define these terms with ease.

Crucial concepts

These are the key terms and concepts you will meet in this Chapter:

Authorised capital	Issued capital
Called-up capital	Losses
Contingent asset	Net assets
Contingent liability	Non-statutory reserves
Depreciation	NRV
Dividends	Paid-up capital
Earnings per share	Share premium a/c
Exceptional items	Shareholders' funds
Gains	Statutory reserves
Intangible fixed assets	Tangible fixed assets

Relevant links

Chapter 8 requires you to use your knowledge of company accounts in evaluating company performance. Chapter 7 shows how another vital financial statement, showing the company's cash flow, is constructed by accountants.

Section I The capital of limited companies

What are you studying?

This Section explains the different types of shares that a company may issue, and how the shareholders are rewarded in the form of a share dividend.

How will you be assessed on this?

To understand company accounts, we need to be familiar with the different forms of share capital, and the basis on which share dividends are calculated. You may be tested by being given information on shares and dividends, asked to calculate the amount of dividend, and record both shares and dividends in the final accounts.

There will also be more demanding questions on capital adjustments and calculations, which are often linked with either accounting ratios or constructing final company accounts.

We have already explained and given examples of these terms, which are particularly relevant to the accounts of limited companies:

- limited liability (page 23);
- separate legal entity (page 23);
- private and public companies (page 24).

The owners of 'ltd' companies and PLCs, who benefit from limited liability and who are distinct from such companies in the eyes of the law are the **shareholders**. The capital of these owners (**proprietors**) in a limited company consists of shares. The **nominal value** ('face value') of these shares will vary, e.g. 10p, 50p, £1.

 Crucial tip

Examiners often set questions where the nominal value of the shares is not £1.

Classifying share capital

Crucial concept

Authorised capital represents the maximum amount of share capital that a limited company can issue; **issued** capital is the amount of share capital actually issued (at its nominal figure); **called-up** capital represents the amount called up per share by the company; and **paid-up** capital is the amount of called-up capital that has actually been paid by shareholders.

- **Authorised**: e.g. 2,000,000 shares of 50p each = £1,000,000 authorised capital.

- **Issued**, e.g. 1,600,000 50p shares issued = £800,000 issued capital.

- **Called-up**, e.g. 1,600,000 50p shares on which the company has called up 25p per share, the called-up capital is £400,000 (the issued capital is still £800,000).

- **Paid-up**, e.g. 1,600,000 50p shares, called-up 25p per share, amount actually paid £390,000 (thus the called-up capital remaining unpaid = £10,000).

 Crucial tip — You need to be quite clear on the nature of capital in a question, especially if you have to calculate the amount of share dividend.

Share premium

The amount (£) at which new shares are issued may be greater than their nominal value. If, for example, a company's £1 shares are trading on the stock market at £1.50, the directors won't issue additional shares for £1, knowing they can get more for each share than this. If, say, they issue 100,000 more shares at £1.40 per share, subscribers will pay £140,000. The company treats this in two ways:

100,000 at £1 nominal value	= £100,000 issued capital
100,000 at 40p excess	= £40,000 share premium

Crucial concept — The **share premium account** records the amount paid over and above the nominal value of the shares.

Declaring dividends and reinvesting profits

The company's managers have to decide how to use the profits made. The fundamental choice they have matches our everyday life choice – whether to spend or save:

- they 'spend' in the sense of **distributing as dividends**;
- they 'save' by **retaining in the company**.

Crucial concept — **Dividends** are appropriations of **taxed** profit.

The company's total dividend may consist of an **interim** and a **final** (also known as **proposed**) dividend.

Interim dividend	Final (proposed) dividend
Declared part-way through the financial year.	Declared at the end of the financial year.
Paid before the end of the year: liability discharged.	**Unpaid** at the end of the year: treated as a current liability.

As an example, if a company has an authorised capital of 4,000,000 25p ordinary shares, and has issued 2,000,000 of these shares, a declared dividend of 6% will cost the company

$$6\% \times £500,000 = £30,000$$

because the **dividend is declared on issued**, rather than authorised, share capital. (Here we can also describe the dividend as '1 ½ p per share'.)

 Crucial tip Questions may state dividend 'per share' or '%'. You therefore need to check carefully the share's nominal value, and the number and value of issued shares.

The company's directors may also decide to **retain** some of the profit as a means of conserving cash to fund development. As we'll see, the P&L account balance is treated as a reserve.

Types of shares

You will meet two main types of shares in company accounts: **ordinary** and **preference**. Table 6.1 lists the main differences between them.

	Preference shares	Ordinary shares
Right to dividend?	Priority over ordinary shareholders	Lowest priority (after preference shareholders)
Right to vote?	No	Yes
Right to repayment of capital?	Priority over ordinary shareholders	Lowest priority (after preference shareholders)
Nature of dividend?	Fixed %	Variable %
Performance in good year?	Typically poor: the 'ceiling' of a fixed dividend	Probably good: a high variable dividend possible
Performance in bad year?	Probably cumulative: dividend can be carried forward to the following year	Typically bad: no surplus profit likely for a dividend (and not cumulative)

Table 6.1 Differences between preference and ordinary shares

The fact that preference shares carry a fixed (e.g. '5% £1 preference') dividend and ordinary shares receive a variable dividend means that the ordinary dividend may fluctuate wildly, depending on profits (and on the ratio of ordinary shares to total capital: see **capital gearing** on page 158).

Crucial concept Ordinary shareholders effectively own and control (by vote) the company, and also own the company's undistributed reserves.

You will be tested on your knowledge that ordinary shares are also known as **equity**.

FRS 14 Earnings per share (EPS)

EPS is an important figure used by actual and potential investors to assess a company's financial performance. Companies must show the EPS figure in their financial statements: by doing so, investors can more easily compare:

- a company's results over time;

- its results with those of different companies.

Crucial concept | **Earnings per share** measures the profit, in pence, per equity (ordinary) share.

Quick check

1. If a company sells 100,000 £5 ordinary shares for £6.50 per share, how much
   (a) share capital
   (b) share premium
   will it receive?

2. How does a company account for an **interim** dividend differently to a **proposed** dividend?

3. Explain **four** differences between ordinary and preference shares.

| Section 2 | The limited company profit and loss account |

What are you studying?

The final accounts of limited companies are fundamentally the same as those for sole traders and partnerships in that:

- the profit and loss account calculates the organisation's net profit made over a period; and

- the balance sheet summarises its financial position as at a particular point in time.

There are many additional complications in company accounts, so we'll start by explaining the categories of one of these financial statements – the profit and loss account – in order to identify some key differences.

How will you be assessed on this?

Much of your assessment in company accounts revolves around your ability to construct a profit and loss account. Questions on the P&L will test your knowledge of its structure, and also your understanding of the way in which profit is both calculated and appropriated. You may also be examined on the way in which relevant FRSs and SSAPs influence the calculations and construction of the P&L (we study FRSs and SSAPs in Section 4).

Here is the layout of a typical profit and loss account containing the major categories required for external (i.e. published) purposes:

	£
Turnover	x
Cost of sales	x
Gross profit	x
Distribution costs	x
Administrative expenses	x
Operating profit	x
Other operating income	x
Interest payable and similar charges	x
Profit on ordinary activities before taxation	x
Taxation on profit on ordinary activities	x
Profit on ordinary activities after taxation	x
Dividends paid and proposed	x
Retained profit	x

The **Notes to the accounts** will include an analysis of **operating profit**: summary information is given on depreciation, auditors' remuneration and directors' emoluments (earnings), research and development and staff costs. The amount of information that must be disclosed overall will depend on the **size** of the company: 'small' and 'medium-sized' companies don't have to include as much detail as the larger companies. To be classed as small or medium-sized, a company needs to meet at least two of the following three conditions:

	Small companies	**Medium-sized companies**
Annual turnover?	Below £2.8 million	Below £11.2 million
Balance sheet total?	Below £1.4 million	Below £5.6 million
Average number of employees?	Below 50	Below 250

 Crucial tip — If you need to memorise these figures, look at their relationship: 1.4 is ½ of 2.8, which is ½ of 5.6, which in turn is ½ of 11.2!

FRS 3

Until fairly recently, there were claims that it was difficult to compare a company's accounts from year to year: for example, turnover and profit figures arising from new activities starting and/or old ones finishing were not always analysed, and it was also possible to manipulate certain figures. As a result, **FRS 3 Reporting Financial Performance** was published.

- Part of FRS 3 identifies three areas for analysis in the P&L:
  - **continuing operations**;
  - **new acquisitions**;
  - **discontinued operations** (e.g. withdrawal from a market or market segment).
- FRS 3 also sets rules for dealing with 'non-ordinary' items, notably those classified as **exceptional items**. (Examples of exceptional items include substantial bad debts and settlement of insurance claims.)

Crucial concept	**Exceptional items** arise from the company's ordinary activities (i.e. an activity undertaken as part of the company's business) but which are disclosed due to their **size** or **incidence**, so the financial statement gives a 'true and fair view'.

- FRS 3 also requires **earnings per share** to be stated.
- Other statements required by FRS 3 are:
  - **Statement of total recognised gains and losses**: this links P&L profit with other gains and losses – an example is **unrealised profits** (e.g. where a fixed asset increases in value such as revaluing property, the gain is recognised but not 'realised' in terms of income or cost).

Statement of total recognised gains and losses	
Profit for the financial year	
(from P&L: profit after tax and extraordinary items)	x
Unrealised surplus …	x
Unrealised loss …	x
Total gains and losses recognised since last annual report	xxx

  - **Reconciliation of movements in shareholders' funds**: this shows why shareholders' funds have changed during the period by focusing on items affecting share capital or reserves (e.g. P&L profit, dividends, new share capital, amortised goodwill).

  - **Note of historical cost profits and losses**: this note is provided if the company has used an alternative valuation approach leading to a material difference in stated profit (that must be reconciled with the historical cost profit figure).

1. State the rules for establishing if a company is 'small' or 'medium-sized'.
2. Explain why FRS 3 was brought into force.

Section 3 · The limited company balance sheet

What are you studying?

You are already familiar with the composition and layout of balance sheets. In company accounts there are some extra items that may feature in a balance sheet, and we also use some different terminology. This Section explains the additional items and new terms.

How will you be assessed on this?

Your examiner may ask you to construct a company balance sheet – often following the P&L – and questions on the balance sheet test not only your knowledge of its structure, but also your understanding of the calculations involved with some of its elements (such as depreciation). You may also be tested on how FRSs and SSAPs influence balance sheet construction.

Chapter 5 introduced us to **goodwill**, which may feature as one of the company's intangible fixed assets. These assets will be **amortised** (depreciated) over their useful lives.

Crucial concept

A company's fixed assets are classified as **intangible** and **tangible**.

You will probably meet these other intangible fixed assets:

- the cost of **patent rights** and **trademarks** (treated as buying an intangible fixed asset);
- **deferred development expenditure**, which occurs where a company can defer (or 'capitalise' as an asset) the cost of developing certain products: see SSAP 13 (page 127).

Tangible fixed assets will be shown, like those of sole traders and partnerships, at **NBV** (net book value, i.e. cost less depreciation). You may find **investments** included as fixed assets if they are regarded as long-term investments; if not, they will be shown with the **current assets**, which are otherwise basically the same as those for sole traders and partnerships.

Current liabilities for a company will include additional items, notably **corporation tax owing** and **proposed dividends**.

Crucial concept

A company's current liabilities are renamed by the 1985 Companies Act as **creditors: amounts falling due within one year**. Long-term liabilities are known as **creditors: amounts falling due after more than one year**.

The major new long-term liability is **debenture stock**, typically known as 'debentures'. This form of **loan capital** differs from share capital in the following ways:

	Debentures	Share capital
Nature of holders?	**Lenders** to the company	**Owners** of the company
Security of holders?	Often **secured** on fixed assets	**Unsecured**
Nature of reward?	**Interest**, paid out of **untaxed** profits (a P&L item)	**Dividend**, paid out of **taxed** profits (an appropriated item)
Entitlement to reward?	Failure to pay, holders can take **legal action** to recover the debt	Shareholders **cannot force payment** of the dividend

Table 6.2 Differences between debentures and share capital

Like share capital, the reward – interest in this case – is calculated on the **nominal value** of the loan stock, and not its market value.

The balance sheet category showing the owners' investment in the company is termed **share capital and reserves**. Details of the share capital – preference and ordinary – are shown, and the **reserves** are then listed.

 Crucial concept — **Statutory** reserves must be set up by a company by law, and cannot be used for the distribution of dividends. **Non-statutory** reserves consist of profits that can be distributed as dividends if the directors so choose.

Retained profits form the main non-statutory reserve, being used as a source for dividends if necessary (in a bad year). Other non-statutory reserves you may come across include the **general reserve** and a **fixed asset replacement reserve**.

Crucial tip — Learn the many other names for retained profits: unappropriated profits, undistributed profits, revenue reserve, retained earnings, and the P&L account balance!

The most important statutory reserve in our studies is the **share premium account**. Page 117 explained how share premium arises as the excess of the issue price of the share over its nominal value. Compared with retained profits, once a share premium account is created it forms part of the company's capital and cannot be used as a source for dividend payment. It can, however, be used for certain purposes such as **issuing bonus shares**.

- If a company builds up sufficient reserves, it may restructure its capital and reserves by converting some of its reserves into share capital.

- The share premium account (or any other reserve) can be used for this purpose.

- The bonus shares are issued to shareholders who now hold more shares.

Note that the total value of their investment is still the same because issuing these bonus shares has not increased the net asset value of the company.

Crucial concept In a company balance sheet, **net assets** = fixed + current assets, less creditors within and longer than one year (current and long-term liabilities). This total equals **shareholders' funds** (i.e. share capital + reserves).

Crucial tip You need to memorise this new terminology for the company balance sheet.

Quick check
1. Name **three** examples of intangible fixed assets.
2. What are the main differences between debentures and share capital?

Section 4 | Important FRSs and SSAPs

What are you studying?

To obtain greater consistency, various accounting 'rules' have been established in recent years. We will study how the major FRSs – Financial Reporting Standards – and SSAPs – Statements of Standard Accounting Practice – influence financial statements.

How will you be assessed on this?

You need to know these rules exist. At this stage of your studies it is unlikely you will be tested in depth on FRSs and SSAPs, but you should be able to incorporate the knowledge you'll gain here when answering descriptive and numerical questions on company accounts.

- We have just studied one of the most important FRSs – **FRS 3 Reporting Financial Performance** (page 121) – and previously learnt how **SSAP 2 Disclosure of Accounting Policies** describes four accounting concepts as 'fundamental' (page 70).

- We will meet other relevant FRSs and SSAPs later, e.g. **FRS 1 Cash flow statements** (Chapter 7).

FRS 10 Goodwill and Intangible Assets

We have already defined goodwill (page 104). FRS 10 requires purchased goodwill and other intangible fixed assets bought by a company to be

capitalised in the balance sheet, and they should normally be **amortised over their useful economic life**. There is an assumption that intangible fixed assets have a life of less than 20 years.

FRS 12 Provisions, Contingent Liabilities and Contingent Assets

This FRS is based on the requirement that a company's financial statements must include all information necessary to understand its financial position. The three items covered by FRS 12 cause problems because they are uncertain in nature.

- **Provisions** (defined on page 76) are treated as **liabilities**, but FRS 12 separates them from other, 'normal' liabilities – creditors, overdrafts and so on – due to provisions being uncertain in both amount and timing.

Crucial concept   A **contingent asset** is an asset arising from past events, but whose existence will not be confirmed until a future event (or events) takes place. A **contingent liability** is a possible obligation arising from past events, but which will not be confirmed until some future event(s) occurs.

Crucial tip   Notice the use of 'possible' in the definition of contingent liabilities: if it is more than 50% probable, we treat it as a provision rather than a contingent liability.

- **Contingent assets** and **contingent liabilities** are therefore 'in the pipeline': they may exist, but we won't know until some further event happens in the future. FRS 12 is influenced by the prudence concept when establishing these rules:
  - a contingent liability is not recognised in the financial statements but needs to be disclosed (by way of a note)
  - a contingent asset is never recognised until its realisation is (virtually) certain.

FRS 15 Tangible Fixed Assets

In our previous Section, we learnt that fixed assets normally appear under three headings:

- **intangible**;
- **tangible**;
- **investments**.

This classification is based on the 1985 Companies Act, which states that **historical cost** should be the basis for recording fixed assets. It also stipulates that any fixed asset having a limited economic life must be subject to **depreciation**.

The 1985 Act makes it possible to use an **alternative basis** – such as their current cost or market values – for revaluing fixed assets, so long as the assets involved and the basis of the valuation are disclosed in the accounts and that the historical cost is also separately disclosed.

- FRS 15 provides rules relating to the initial measurement, revaluation and depreciation of tangible fixed assets, and in terms of what needs to be disclosed concerning this:
  - a tangible fixed asset should initially be **measured at cost** (i.e. cost of buying it plus cost of getting it into working condition, such as site clearance, installation costs);
  - if the company has a policy on revaluing tangible fixed assets, this policy must be **used consistently** with all assets of the same type (gains and losses on revaluation will be reported in the statement of total recognised gains and losses. See page 121);
  - depreciation is viewed under FRS 15 as a method for allocating the cost of the asset over a number of accounting periods (i.e. the accruals concept).

Crucial concept   A more detailed definition of **depreciation** (see also page 76) is that it measures the cost, or revalued amount of the economic benefits, of a tangible fixed asset as a result of it being **consumed** (wearing out through use, passage of time, obsolescence) during a given period.

  - FRS 15 does not stipulate which method must be used to calculate depreciation. What it does make clear is that any **change** from one method to another is only allowable if the new method gives a **fairer presentation** of the financial position.

SSAP 5 Accounting for VAT

VAT is a tax associated with the supply of goods and services and requiring businesses to deal with HM Customs and Excise. SSAP 5 sets these rules:

- turnover and cost of sales shown in P&L should exclude VAT;
- the amount due to HM Customs and Excise is shown in the total for creditors – if a net amount is owed by HM Customs and Excise, this is shown in the total debtors figure.

SSAP 9 Stocks and Long-Term Contracts

Crucial concept   SSAP 9 states that stock should be **valued at the lower of cost or NRV** (net realisable value).

- 'Cost' here includes not only the cost of buying the goods, but also related costs such as transport;
- 'NRV' is calculated by taking the known or estimated selling price, less

any further completion and selling/distribution costs.

- SSAP 9 also considers the **methods** for valuing stock, stating that LIFO and replacement cost should not normally be used.
  - **FIFO** (first in, first out): when stock is issued, the 'first in' (i.e. oldest) price is selected and used.
  - **LIFO** (last in, first out): the most recent price is used to cost the stock when it is issued from stores.
  - **AVCO** (average cost): as each stock consignment arrives, the average purchase price for all the stock in stores is recalculated, this price then being used when stock is issued for production.
  - **Replacement cost**: when stock is issued, its replacement (i.e. current) cost is identified and used.
  - **Standard cost**: if the company has a standard costing system, the standard cost of the stock can be used to price it.

 Crucial tip   FIFO and AVCO are the most popular methods found in practice.

SSAP 13 Accounting for Research and Development

Companies undertaking research and development (R&D) must decide how to treat this cost: as an **expense**, i.e. written off in P&L, or as an **asset** (shown in the balance sheet). Why treat R&D expenditure as an asset? The argument is that R&D generates future sales revenue, so the related costs can be 'capitalised' and spread across the same accounting periods (the accruals concept) to which these increased sales apply.

SSAP 13 classifies R&D expenditure under three headings, as shown in Table 6.3.

Pure (original) research	Applied research	Development expenditure
This research has no obvious commercial end-product.	This has a more practical purpose.	This focuses on producing specific new/improved products.
These forms of research are regarded as being necessary for the company's continuing survival. They are written off as costs in the year in which they are incurred.		This cost is closely related to expectations of profit. This cost can be capitalised as a deferred asset and written off (amortised) against future revenues.

Table 6.3 Classifications of R&D

Quick check

1. Explain the difference between a contingent liability and a contingent asset.
2. Define 'depreciation'.
3. Explain the difference between FIFO, LIFO and AVCO.

Section 5	The ASB's *Statement of Principles*

What are you studying?

The Accounting Standards Board (ASB) published this *Statement* in December 1999.

How will you be assessed on this?

As you continue to study accounting in greater depth, you will need to be familiar with the background and development of accounting principles. It's therefore important to be at least aware of the current developments taking place, and it's quite possible that you will be tested on your knowledge of developments such as this *Statement*.

The ASB *Statement* was developed for a number of reasons:

- to increase consistency and objectivity in reporting financial accounting;
- to support future development of various accounting standards;
- to support the work of external and internal auditors; and
- to help users of financial statements interpret them.

As we mentioned in Chapter 1, financial statements need to be:

- consistent;
- clear;
- informative.

The ASB's *Statement* defines the **objective of financial statements**.

Crucial concept

'The objective of financial statements is to provide information about the financial **position**, **performance** and financial **adaptability** of an enterprise that is useful to a wide range of users for assessing the stewardship of management and for making economic decisions.'

- Chapter 1 has already described the various users of these statements and explained (page 27) the nature of 'the stewardship of management': exercise 3 at the end of the Chapter also tested your knowledge on financial (economic) decisions.
- Chapter 4 gives the ASB definition of the main elements of financial statements. Additional definitions are given in the *Statement* for gains, losses, contributions from and distributions to owners.

 **Crucial concept**   **Gains** are increases – and **losses** are decreases – in ownership interest, other than those relating to contributions from owners. **Contributions from owners** are increases – and **distributions to owners** are decreases – in ownership interest resulting from investments made by owners.

The *Statement* also provides information on the presentation of financial information. The chapter identifies **primary financial statements** as:

- the profit and loss account;
- the balance sheet;
- the statement of total recognised gains and losses;
- the cash flow statement.

Quick check
1. What **three** key qualities should financial statements possess?
2. List and describe (a) the users of, and (b) the elements in, financial statements.

Crucial examples

1. Merchant Magic Ltd has an authorised capital of 100,000 7% £1 preference shares, and 1 million ordinary shares of 50p each. It has issued all its preference shares, and 750,000 ordinary shares.

   Profits after tax for the year to 30 June 2002 were £148,500. The board of directors has declared and paid an interim dividend of 4% per ordinary share. The board has now declared that the preference dividend will be paid in full, and that there will be a final ordinary dividend of 6% per share.

   Calculate and state:
   (a) the preference and ordinary dividends;
   (b) the amount of profit retained in the company;
   (c) the earnings per share (in pence) for the ordinary shares;
   (d) any liabilities as a result of the above.

2. Here are extracted balances from the books of Gabriel Ltd, on 31 December 2002:

	£000	£000
Stock (1.1.2002)	54	
Sales		280
Purchases	74	
Office salaries	47	
Office expenses	24	
Distribution salaries	36	
Distribution expenses	16	

	£000	£000
Commission received		8
Income from investments		12
Depreciation: buildings	10	
office equipment	5	
motor vehicles	10	
Debenture interest	15	
Interim dividend	6	
Profit and loss balance (1.1.2002)		595

Additional information:
(a) stocks at 31.12.2002 are £75,000;
(b) taxation on profit from ordinary activities is £37,000;
(c) buildings depreciation is allocated 60% office, 40% distribution;
(d) issued share capital consists of 100,000 ordinary shares of £1 each; the directors have proposed a final dividend of 8p per share.

Prepare the company's profit and loss account.

3. After completing the profit and loss account for the year to 30 September 2002, the accountant of Edwood Ltd had the following trial balance:

	£000	£000
Debtors and creditors	172	75
Provision for doubtful debts (1.10.2001)		15
Bank	32	
Prepaid expenses	3	
Share premium account		30
Corporation tax		25
Stock (30.9.2002)	115	
Property (cost)	400	
Vehicles (cost)	120	
Provisions for depreciation of: property		50
vehicles		77
Investments	153	
8% debenture stock		200
Proposed ordinary dividend		25
Profit and loss account balance		98
Ordinary share capital		400
	995	995

The company's authorised and issued capital is 2,000,000 ordinary shares of 25p each.

Prepare the company's balance sheet.

4. (a) Under Companies Acts legislation, limited companies must disclose accounting policies in the notes to their accounts. Explain why this is important, referring to
   (i) stock (SSAP 9)
   (ii) research and development (SSAP 13)
   (iii) depreciation (FRS 15)
   in your answer.
   (b) A new company director has noticed certain changes in the company's final accounts, and has asked you to answer this question: 'The shares issued this year were issued at a premium of 10p each: why?'

5. Explain each of these terms:

Authorised capital	Issued capital
Called-up capital	Losses
Contingent asset	Net assets
Contingent liability	Non-statutory reserves
Depreciation	NRV
Dividends	Paid-up capital
Earnings per share	Share premium a/c
Exceptional items	Shareholders' funds
Gains	Statutory reserves
Intangible fixed assets	Tangible fixed assets

Answers

1. (a) Preference dividend = 7% of £100,000 = £7,000 out of profits.
   Ordinary dividend: interim = 2p × 750,000 = £15,000.
   proposed = 3p × 750,000 = £22,500.
   (Be careful to calculate % per share, e.g. 4% of 50p = 2p.)
   (b) Retained profits = £148,500 − (£7,000 + £15,000 + £22,500) = £104,500.
   (c) Earnings per ordinary share = 5p (10% of 50p nominal share value).
   (d) Proposed preference and ordinary dividends are current liabilities (£29,500); the retained profits of £104,500 form part of the reserves.

2. **Gabriel Ltd**

Profit and loss account for year ending 31 December 2002

	£000
Turnover	280
Cost of sales (54 + 74 − 75)	(53)
Gross profit	227
Distribution costs (36 + 16 + 10 + 4 buildings depr.)	(66)
Administrative expenses (47 + 24 + 5 + 6 buildings depr.)	(82)
Operating profit	79

	£000
Other operating income (12 + 8)	20
Interest payable and similar charges	(15)
Profit on ordinary activities before taxation	84
Taxation on profit on ordinary activities	(37)
Profit on ordinary activities after taxation	47
Dividends paid and proposed (6 interim + 8 final)	(14)
Retained profit	33

3.

Edwood Ltd

Balance sheet as at 30 September 2002

	£000 Cost	£000 Depr	£000 Net
Fixed assets:			
Property	400	50	350
Vehicles	120	77	43
Investments			153
			546
Current assets:			
Stock		115	
Debtors	172		
Provision for doubtful debts	15	157	
Prepaid expenses		3	
Bank		32	
		307	
Creditors: amounts falling due within one year:			
Creditors	75		
Corporation tax	25		
Proposed ordinary dividend	25	125	
Net current assets			182
			728
Creditors: amounts falling due after more than one year:			
8% debenture loan stock			(200)
Net assets			528
Capital and reserves:			
Authorised and issued ordinary share capital			400
Share premium account			30
Profit and loss account			98
			528

4. (a) (i) SSAP 9 requires that stock must be valued at the lower of cost or NRV. Because stock is a material figure, the basis of its valuation must be given in order for users of the statements to see how the final figure is arrived at.

(ii) SSAP 13 requires 'pure' and 'applied' research costs to be written off as revenue expenditure to the year in question. Development costs, if they meet certain stated criteria, can be capitalised and deferred to future years, being offset against the extra revenues generated as a result of the development. It is important to explain the nature of these costs.

(Iii) FRS 15 requires the cost of depreciation to be spread over the useful life of the associated asset. Since there are a number of different ways to calculate depreciation, the one(s) used by the organisation need clarifying in the notes.

(b) This has occurred because the shares were issued at a price above their nominal (face) value. The extra amount over and above the nominal value has to be credited to a share premium account.

5. Check your answers against the **Crucial concepts** in the chapter.

Crucial reading and research

Reading

These books provide more information on the final accounts of companies:

Dodge, R. (1997) *Foundations of Business Accounting*, 2nd edn. International Thomson Business Press (ISBN 1 86512 153 7). See Chapter 10, 'Limited companies: capital and reserves', and Chapter, 1 'Limited companies: accounting regulations'.

Dyson, J. R. (1994) *Accounting for Non-Accounting Students*, 3rd edn. Pitman Publishing (ISBN 0 273 60435 X). See Chapter 6, 'Limited companies' (pp. 134–47).

Glautier, M. W. E. and Underdown, B. (1997) *Accounting Theory and Practice*, 6th edn. Pitman Publishing (ISBN 0 273 62444 X). See Chapter 13, 'Companies: their nature and regulation', and Chapter 14, 'Published financial statements'.

Research

This chapter has covered some of the most influential FRSs and SSAPs, but there are many others. FRSs are gradually replacing SSAPs, so it's important to keep checking if there are any changes being made to the ones outlined in the Chapter. Also, explore some of the other accounting rules that may be particularly relevant to your own background and studies. For example, if you have experience or involvement with one company in a group, here are some relevant FRSs:

- FRS 2 Accounting for Subsidiary Undertakings
- FRS 6 Acquisitions and Mergers

- FRS 9 Associates and Joint Ventures

Finally, take whatever opportunity you can to continue looking at published company accounts. Although these accounts will contain far more detail than you need to understand at present, you will be able to see the relationship between what you've just studied and what happens in real life.

CHAPTER 7

CASH FLOW STATEMENTS

Chapter summary

This Chapter provides the setting for an important financial statement – in some ways, the most important of all statements. Companies must prepare cash flow statements, and all businesses should also prepare them in view of the information they display. These statements inform managers and other users of financial information about the nature of the organisation's cash inflows and outflows: the users can gauge from this information some indication of the organisation's likely chances of survival.

Studying this Chapter will help you to:

- understand the difference between profit and cash flows;

- describe the structure of a cash flow statement such as the format used in FRS 1;

- calculate the net cash inflow from trading activities; and

- construct a full cash flow statement.

Assessment targets

Target I: explaining the difference between cash flow and profit
You will have to be aware of this difference. Exercise I at the end of the Chapter tests your awareness.

Target 2: reconciling profit and cash flow
You have to not only know the difference (in Target I), but also how to calculate this difference. Exercise 2 at the end of the Chapter tests your ability to distinguish between, and to reconcile, profit and cash flow.

Target 3: constructing a full cash flow statement
In your assessment, you will be given a set of final accounts and asked to use this information in order to construct a cash flow statement. This Chapter contains a worked example, which will take you through the construction of such a statement on a step-by-step basis. Exercise 3 at the end of the Chapter also assesses your ability to do this.

Target 4: using accounting terms appropriately
You will have to use the terms associated with cash flow statements appropriately. Exercise 4 at the end of the Chapter assesses whether you can define these terms with ease.

Crucial concepts

These are the key terms and concepts you will meet in this Chapter:

Cash flow statement	Liquidity
Depreciation	Reconciliation

Relevant links

To study this Chapter effectively, you need to be aware of how final accounts are constructed (Chapters 2 and 3) and the nature of these final accounts (in particular, company accounts – see Chapter 6).

Section I	The difference between cash and profit

What are you studying?

You have come across reported cash and reported profit figures, and there may be an assumption made that an increase in cash means an equivalent increase in profit. This isn't the case, and so in this Section you'll learn more about how and why there is a difference between cash and profit.

How will you be assessed on this?

You need to know what causes changes in the cash balance. Your exam or coursework may ask you to construct a cash flow statement, which will analyse the amount by which, and why, the period's closing cash balance differs from the opening one. Such questions are based on the various ways in which companies use cash and the workings of the accruals concept. Questions on cash flow statements may test your knowledge of the requirements of, and layout required by, FRS I.

Why do businesses need to display their cash movements in detail? Surely a profit and loss account gives a sufficient indication of how successful the business is? No it doesn't!

- A company's managers are interested in its chances of **survival**. In the short term at least, this relies more on an ability to meet debts as they fall due rather than on its ability to make profits. **Liquidity** is all important, and is not clearly illustrated by the level of profits made.

Crucial concept   **Liquidity** (see also page 26) is a measure of an organisation's ability to meet cash-based commitments, such as paying its debts or paying the shareholders' dividend.

- A profit figure therefore may give a **misleading indication** of cash flow and liquidity, e.g. shareholders, when seeing the company's profit-after-tax figure, may think that substantial dividends can be paid, but this is only possible if the company has sufficient cash.

What causes the different movements of cash and profit?

- **The accruals concept** (page 42). Revenues and expenses (i.e. gains and losses) are matched to the periods to which they refer, whereas cash is simply accounted for as and when it is received and paid.

- **Capital and revenue expenditure** (page 41). The P&L only accounts for revenue expenditure, whereas the cash balance is affected by capital financing and capital expenditure (i.e. changes in balance sheet items).

Crucial tip   Revisit the content of both P&L and balance sheet to explore the reasons for the difference between cash and profit movements.

The ways in which cash flow differs from profit, and the main headings for analysing cash flow, are contained in FRS I.

Quick check   Give **three** examples of where a change in the cash balance will not be reflected by an equal change in the amount of profit/loss.

Section 2	FRS I

What are you studying?   In this Section you'll learn about the requirements that FRS I *Cash Flow Statements* makes regarding the structure of a published cash flow statement.

How will you be assessed on this?   Questions on cash flow statements will require you to use and understand the various headings found in FRS I. You will be tested on your ability to categorise cash figures using appropriate headings, and to adjust these figures (e.g. as a result of the workings of the accruals concept).

 Crucial concept   **FRS I Cash flow statements** establishes the structure of cash flow statements for companies.

FRS I requires companies to report their cash flow movements using the main headings shown in Table 7.1.

I.	**Operating activities**	Here, the cash generated by trading transactions is shown: we show how important making profit is in increasing the cash balance. We will also study a related reconciliation between the 'net cash flow from operating activities' with 'operating profit'.
2.	**Returns on investment and servicing of finance**	'Returns on investment' are cash inflows for interest and dividends received; 'servicing of finance' represents cash outflows for interest and dividends paid. *The company's equity (ordinary share) dividends are dealt with under the separate heading below.*
3.	**Taxation**	Here we record tax movements, notably corporation tax payments made to the tax authorities.
4.	**Capital expenditure and financial investment**	The cash flow here relates to payments to acquire fixed assets and any cash received from the sale of fixed assets.
5.	**Acquisitions and disposals**	This category records any cash flow as a result of acquiring, or disposing of, any businesses owned by the organisation.
6.	**Equity dividends paid**	This category shows the outflow of cash in the form of ordinary share dividends.
7.	**Management of liquid resources**	Here we state cash flow to do with resources such as short-term deposits or any other 'liquid' (i.e. 'near-cash') investments.
8.	**Financing**	Cash inflows include receipts from share and debenture issues; cash outflows include repaying shares and long-term loans.

Table 7.I Cash flow statements: Main headings

Crucial tip   While you may not be required to memorise these headings, it is useful to try to do so; the categories will then become much more familiar to you.

FRS I also requires two **reconciliations** to be shown.

 A **reconciliation** occurs when two figures are linked together logically.

- The reconciliation between operating profit and net cash flow from operating activities (mentioned in Table 7.1) analyses how non-cash and current asset movements have caused the difference between the P&L operating profit and the cash flow shown in the statement.

- The movement in cash in the period and the movement in net debt is also reconciled.

 Crucial tip   The first reconciliation is probably more important for your studies at this level.

Quick check   1. List and describe the main headings required by FRS I.
2. Name the **two** reconciliation statements drawn up to supplement the cash flow statement.

Section 3   Reconciling cash and operating profit

What are you studying?

This Section takes what you have learnt in the previous Sections and uses it to reconcile the cash and operating profit figures that you're given.

How will you be assessed on this?

In questions on cash flow statements, whether or not based on the requirements of FRS I, you will be tested on your ability to calculate the cash figure generated for the organisation through its trading activities. To answer these questions or sections, you need to memorise and apply a set procedure to 'translate' the income from profit into its equivalent cash inflow.

We'll use the following final accounts to illustrate how this is done.

Murphy Ltd
Profit and loss account for year ended 31 December 2001

	£000
Turnover	8,909
Cost of sales	(4,102)
Gross profit	4,807
Profit on sale of fixed asset	68
Depreciation	(885)
Other expenses	(900)

	£000
Operating profit for the year	3,090
Interest paid	(310)
Profit before tax	2,780
Tax	(945)
Profit after tax	1,835
Ordinary dividend	(500)
Retained profit	1,335

Balance sheet as at 31 December 2001

	2001		2000	
	£000	£000	£000	£000
Fixed assets (net)		7,500		6,960
Current assets:				
Stocks	2,850		3,286	
Trade debtors	1,842		1,464	
Cash	405		300	
	5,097		5,050	
Current liabilities:				
Trade creditors	820		655	
Dividends payable	360		345	
Tax payable	945		873	
	2,125		1,873	
Net current assets		2,972		3,177
Long-term loan		(4,400)		(6,400)
Net assets		6,072		3,737
Capital and reserves:				
Called-up share capital		2,500		2,000
Share premium		600		100
Profit and loss account		2,972		1,637
		6,072		3,737

Additional information: a fixed asset costing £250,000 with accumulated depreciation of £85,000 was sold during the year.

Prepare a cash flow statement for the year ended 31 December 2001.

Calculating net cash inflow from operating activities

The standard procedure is to follow and complete this layout, starting with operating profit and finishing with its cash flow equivalent for 2001:

£000

Operating profit	
Add depreciation charge for the year	
Less profit (add loss) on sale of fixed assets	
Adjust for current assets/liabilities other than cash:	
Stock (add decrease/deduct increase)	
Debtors (add decrease/deduct increase)	
Creditors (add increase/deduct decrease)	_____
Net cash inflow from operating activities	_____

Starting with the operating profit (£3,200), we add back the depreciation charged in P&L.

 Crucial concept   **Depreciation** (see also page 76) is a non-cash expense.

 Crucial tip   Because depreciation is a non-cash expense, it will reduce profit, but doesn't have any effect on cash flow; to get the 'cash equivalent' we therefore add depreciation back to operating profit.

We also adjust for any profit/loss on the sale of fixed assets. Like depreciation, these are book-keeping adjustments that affect profit but don't affect cash flow. (The profit on the sale of the fixed asset is also shown in the P&L account.)

Finally, we calculate the changes in the remaining current assets and current liabilities over the year and either add or subtract them. An increase in a current asset – we'll use stock as an illustration – equals an equivalent decrease in cash, and vice versa (stock increase = more at end of year than at start = we have managed to preserve cash equal to this amount).

Similarly, an increase in a current liability equates to an increase in cash, and vice versa. If, for example, creditors have fallen over the year, this means that – relatively speaking – we have paid more cash out during the year, amounting to a net reduction in the cash balance.

 Crucial tip   Note that we don't at this stage account for dividends and tax: you learnt in the last Section that FRS I deals with these items under different headings.

Quick check   Complete the above reconciliation statement using the figures from Murphy Ltd's final accounts.

What are you studying?

This Section takes what you have calculated in the last Section, and uses it in the full cash flow statement. (We simplify the figures by ignoring '000' in the workings.)

How will you be assessed on this?

When answering full questions on cash flow statements, you'll take your calculation of cash flow from operating activities and include it as one of the main figures in the statement. Again, you may be tested on your memory of the various headings, and will certainly have to identify and adjust relevant figures in the final accounts, in order to complete the cash flow statement.

....

What answer did you arrive at in the last **Quick check**? You should have the following:

	£000	
Operating profit	3,090	taken from the P&L
Add depreciation	885	again taken from the P&L
Less profit on sale of fixed assets	(68)	from P&L (see note)
Decrease in stock	436	from balance sheet (3,286 fallen to 2,850)
Increase in debtors	(378)	from balance sheet (1,464 increased to 1,842)
Increase in creditors	165	from balance sheet (655 increased to 820)
Net cash inflow from operating activities	4,130	

Note: The profit on sale of fixed assets has increased the profit figure, but the cash from the sale is picked up in the fixed asset calculations (study page 143) and not here, so the profit is deducted (any loss would be added).

What are we looking for overall? If you check the balance sheet, you'll see that cash has increased by £105, from £300 to £405. This increase in cash is the figure we'll be looking for in the cash flow statement. We've already calculated the first figure needed: net cash flow from operating activities amounting to £4,130.

 Crucial tip   Now try recalling the other headings in the cash flow statement.

Returns on investments and servicing of finance

You need to check for any interest/dividend received and paid by the company. The P&L shows a figure of £310 for interest paid, which is the figure we need for the statement.

 Crucial tip   Don't forget that at this stage we ignore any equity dividends, since they have their own heading.

Taxation

We need to find the amount paid in tax during 2001. The P&L shows a figure of £945 for corporation tax, but this does **not** represent the cash paid because it is the amount of tax still owing at the end of December 2001. It is shown in this year's account (the accruals concept) since it represents this year's tax charge, but it will be paid **next** year. The proof is in the balance sheet, where £945 is shown as tax still **payable**.

The cash figure for tax paid this year comes from the balance sheet figure for 2000: the tax payable at the end of 2000 has been paid in 2001, so we choose £873 as the figure for the statement.

Capital expenditure

We use the 'logic' used to calculate the last two figures to help us calculate amounts paid for, and received from the sale of, fixed assets. First, let's check how much money we received from the sale of the asset mentioned in the note underneath the final accounts.

- The net book value (NBV) for this asset is £165 (250 cost less 85 depreciation).
- But we've made £67 profit on selling the asset (the 'profit on sale' figure in P&L).
- This profit means we've received £67 more cash than the NBV figure.
- So cash received from the sale = £165 + £67 = £233.

The cash paid for the fixed assets bought seems deceptively easy to work out because the fixed assets figure has increased by £540 (7,500 − 6,960). However, this is a **net** increase, and doesn't take into account the NBV of the asset sold and the effect of depreciation on the closing balance of £7,500. Thus:

- The opening balance includes the asset sold during the year; the closing figure doesn't − deduct the £165 NBV from the opening figure to compare like with like;
- The closing figure has been reduced by the annual depreciation: add back to see the increase in fixed assets at cost.
- Opening £6,960 − £165 = £6,795; closing £7,500 + £885 depreciation = £8,385.
- Value of fixed assets bought (i.e. cash outlay) = £8,385 − £6,795 = £1,590.

The net figure for capital expenditure in the cash flow statement is £1,590 − £233 = £1,357.

Equity dividends paid

Just when you thought it could only get easier, we still have to adjust this figure due to the accruals concept. The P&L shows £500 equity dividends, but – like taxation – this doesn't mean cash paid. Although there could be an interim (i.e. paid) dividend included in this figure, there will be a closing current liability of dividends owing to shareholders at the year end.

Checking the balance sheet confirms that some of this is still owing at the end of 2001 (i.e. £360). How we calculate the cash paid for ordinary dividends during 2001 is as follows:

- Dividends owed at end of last year = £345.
- Dividends declared during this year = £500.
- Therefore total dividends payable = £845.
- But amount still owing at end of this year = £360.
- So amount actually paid to ordinary shareholders = £845 – £360 = £485.

This is the figure representing cash paid as equity dividends that we need for the statement.

Financing

We get our final figure by checking the movements of capital and long-term loans. You can see from the balance sheet that:

- share capital has increased by £500;
- the share premium account has also increased by £500; and
- the long-term loan has fallen by £2,000.

You know that the share premium account increases as a result of issuing capital at above its nominal value, so an increase in share premium means an increase in cash in the same way that an increase in share capital equals an increase in cash.

The figure we therefore need for the statement is £500 + £500 – £2,000.

 Quick check

Complete the cash flow statement, using the FRS 1 headings and the amounts calculated above.

| Section 5 | **Summarising cash flow** |

What are you studying?

This Section ties together what you've studied on cash flow to date.

How will you be assessed on this?

You will need not only to calculate the correct figures for your cash flow statement, but also to state whether the figure has led to an increase or a reduction in the cash balance. Questions on cash flow statements therefore require you to summarise your workings, and to state the net cash change.

What answer did you arrive at for the last **Quick check**? Your cash flow statement should read as follows:

Murphy Ltd
Cash flow statement for year ended 31 December 2001 (don't forget the title!)

	£000	£000	
Net cash inflows from operating activities		4,130	see page 142
Returns on investment and servicing of finance:			
Interest paid		(310)	cash outflow, so negative
Taxation		(873)	cash outflow
Capital expenditure:			
Payments for tangible fixed assets	(1,590)		
Receipt from sale of tangible fixed assets	233		
Net cash outflow from capital expenditure		(1,357)	cash outflow
Equity dividends paid		(485)	cash outflow
Financing:			
Receipts from issue of share capital	1,000		
Payment of long-term loan	(2,000)		
Net cash outflows from financing		(1,000)	cash outflow
Increase in cash during year		105	(i.e. 405 – 300: see page 142)

 Crucial tip Many students get the (difficult) calculations correct, then forget the (easy) classifying of inflows as **plus** and outflows as **minus**.

 Quick check For each of the above totals, explain why it represents either a cash inflow or a cash outflow.

Crucial examples

1. (a) Are the following statements true or false?
   - (i) Paying tax reduces the cash position.
   - (ii) Depreciation reduces the cash position.
   - (iii) A decrease in debtors decreases the cash position.
   - (iv) An increase in creditors increases the cash position.
   - (v) Increase in cash £2,000 always equals increase in profit £2,000.

   (b) Define the terms 'capital expenditure' and 'revenue expenditure', and explain whether each or both causes a difference between profits and cash flows.

2. These are the financial statements of King Ltd.

King Ltd
Profit and loss account for the year ended 31 December

	2001	2000
	£000	£000
Turnover	2,697	2,335
Cost of sales	1,442	1,313
Gross profit	1,255	1,022
Depreciation	153	128
Other expenses	496	445
Loss on sale of fixed assets	4	11
Operating profit for the year	602	438
Interest payable	75	85
Profit before tax	527	353
Tax on profits	287	181
Profit after tax	240	172
Ordinary dividend	100	80
Retained profits	140	92

King Ltd
Balance sheet as at 31 December

	2001	2000
	£000	£000
Fixed assets	2,800	2,558
Current assets:		
Stocks	532	481
Debtors	572	577
Cash	–	23
Current liabilities:		
Creditors	364	469
Dividends payable	100	80
Tax payable	275	202
Bank overdraft	137	–
Long-term loan	680	880
	2,348	2,008
Capital and reserves:		
Share capital	1,800	1,600
Profit and loss account	548	408
	2,348	2,008

Note: Fixed assets costing £265,000 and having accumulated depreciation of £128,000 were sold during the year for £133,000.

Construct a statement reconciling cash flows from operating activities with operating profit.

3. Use the financial statements in, and your answer from, Exercise 2 to construct a full cash flow statement for King Ltd.

4. Define each of these terms:

Cash flow statement	Liquidity
Depreciation	Reconciliation

Answers

1. (a) (i) and (iv) true; (ii), (iii) and (v) false.

(b) Capital expenditure is the purchase of new (or improvement of existing) fixed assets: as such, it affects cash flow but not profit except for the depreciation charge against profits (as a non-cash expense, depreciation as such does not affect cash-flow). Revenue expenditure records normal running expenses, e.g. paying wages, and as such affects both profit and cash flow: applying the accruals concept may lead to a difference between profit and cash flow as a result of this expenditure.

2.
King Ltd
Reconciliation of cash flows from operating activities with operating profit

	£000
Operating profit	602
Depreciation	153
Loss on sale of fixed assets	4
Increase in stocks	(51)
Decrease in debtors	5
Decrease in creditors	(105)
Net cash flow from operating activities	608

3.
King Ltd
Cash flow statement for year ended 31 December 2001

	£000	£000	Notes
Net cash inflow from operating activities		608	See above
Returns on investment and servicing of finance		(75)	P&L figure
Taxation		(214)	See note 1
Capital expenditure:			
Payments for purchase of fixed assets	(532)		See note 2
Receipts from sale of fixed assets	133	(399)	See note 3
Equity dividends paid		(80)	Last year's dividend
Financing:			
Receipts from share capital	200		
Repayment of loan capital	(200)	–	
Decrease in cash		160	

Notes:

'Proof' of decrease = £23 in 2000 balance sheet becoming £137 overdraft in 2001.

1. Tax paid = £202 opening balance + £287 P&L − £275 closing balance.
2. Purchase of fixed assets: £2,800 closing balance + £153 depreciation = £2,953. £2,558 opening balance − £137 NBV (265 − 128) = £2,421; purchase = £2,953 − £2,421 = £532.
3. Receipts from sale given as £133 (i.e. £137 NBV − £4 loss on sale).

4. Check your answers against the **Crucial concepts** in the Chapter.

Crucial reading and research

Reading

These books provide more information on cash flow statements:

Dodge, R. (1997) *Foundations of Business Accounting*, 2nd edn. International Thomson Business Press (ISBN 1 86512 153 7). See Chapter 11, 'Cash flow statements'.

Dyson, J. R. (1994) *Accounting for Non-Accounting Students*. 3rd edn. Pitman Publishing (ISBN 0 273 60435 X). See Chapter 7, 'Cash flow statements'.

Glautier, M. W. E. and Underdown, B. (1997) *Accounting Theory and Practice*, 6th edn. Pitman Publishing (ISBN 0 273 62444 X). See Chapter 15, 'Cash flow statements'.

Wood, F. and Sangster, A. (1999) *Business Accounting 1*, 8th edn. Financial Times/Pitman Publishing (ISBN 0 273 63742 8). See Chapter 38, 'Cash flow statements'.

Research

We suggest three ways to take your knowledge further. First, in this Chapter we've outlined the key points from FRS 1, but if you are required to have a more in-depth knowledge of cash flow statements, study this FRS fully.

What will also help you learn more about cash flow statements is to continue reading and studying those published accounts we've already suggested you get hold of, which will include examples of these statements.

Finally, if necessary, use the above texts and your published accounts to study the nature of the other reconciliations that are constructed to support the main cash flow statement.

CHAPTER 8

RATIO
ANALYSIS

Chapter summary

The role of the accountant is not only to record transactions, but also to report on the organisation's financial performance to management. This Chapter provides the framework for analysing and interpreting this performance by describing, explaining and showing how to calculate the main accounting ratios.

Studying this Chapter will help you to:

- classify and describe the purpose of the main types of accounting ratio;
- calculate these ratios from given information;
- consider and comment on the results of your calculations; and
- use ratio-related accounting terms appropriately.

Assessment targets

Target I: calculating ratios

In your assessment, you may be given a set of accounts and be asked to calculate relevant ratios. Exercises I and 2 at the end of the Chapter assess your ability to do this.

Target 2: explaining the results of your calculations

You will have to use the information from your calculations in order to make judgements about an organisation's financial position and performance. Exercises I and 2 at the end of the Chapter also test you on this.

Target 3: using accounting terms appropriately

Throughout your assessments, you will have to use ratio-related terms appropriately. Exercise 3 at the end of the Chapter assesses whether you can define these terms with ease.

Crucial concepts

These are the key terms associated with ratios that you'll meet in this Chapter:

Asset turnover	Efficiency
Creditor days	Gearing
Current	GP margin
Debt	Interest cover
Debt–equity	Investment
Debtor days	NP margin
Dividend cover	Quick assets
Dividend yield	ROCE
Earnings yield	Stockturn
EPS	Window dressing

Relevant links

You've already studied how various final accounts are created in Chapters 4–6. We use these final accounts as the main information source for calculating accounting ratios.

Section I	**Types of ratios**

What are you studying?

We calculate accounting ratios to analyse financial statements. Although these statements have to be prepared (e.g. as a legal requirement), they provide information on the firm's financial performance, the results being used for inter-firm comparisons and to identify trends.

This Section introduces you to the main categories of ratios.

How will you be assessed on this?

Descriptive questions on this topic may ask you to explain the nature and importance of ratio analysis. Most questions are computational, testing you on your ability to assess, and to communicate the results of this assessment of, the financial performance of a given firm. To do this, the question normally gives you a set of summarised final accounts from which you calculate relevant ratios. It isn't only a question of calculation, however: most of the marks are usually awarded for your ability to reach and communicate your interpretation of the results.

What do we already know? The **users** of financial information are internal and/or external to the firm, and each has a special interest in the firm's performance.

Internal group:	Interest:
• **Managers**	Financial situation: to control, to take decisions. The main areas of interest are profitability, liquidity and asset efficiency.
• **Employees**	The firm's financial situation: this influences job prospects, pay claims, profit-sharing etc.
• **Shareholders**	To evaluate the effectiveness of the financial stewardship.

External group:	Interest:
• **Government agencies**	Inland Revenue (profits), HM Customs & Excise (VAT); information on overall performance for national statistics.
• **Lenders**	To ensure interest and/or credit payments will be met.
• **Analysts**	Information for their clients.
• **Traders**	Assessing whether the firm is a safe supply source.
• **Public**	If the firm is suitable for investment.

Crucial concept

The results of the analysis are used to compare the current performance of the firm against:

- that of its **competitors**, to examine its relative competitiveness;
- its **own performance** in past years, to identify any trends.

Categories of ratios

Many of the ratios assess the firm's **profitability** (page 25) or its **liquidity** (page 26). Other ratios either assess the firm's **efficiency** or are related to **investment** in it.

Crucial concept

Efficiency ratios are used to help assess how efficient the firm is in using its resources. **Investment ratios** are used to assess the value and worth of investing in the firm by shareholders and/or other investors.

Table 8.I provides a summary of the main ratios we will study in the next four sections.

Profitability	Liquidity	Efficiency	Investment
ROCE	Current ratio	Asset turnover	EPS
GP margin	Quick assets	Debtor days	Dividend per share
NP margin	Debt ratio	Creditor days	Dividend cover
	Gearing	Stockturn	P/E ratio
	Debt/equity		Dividend yield
	Interest cover		Earnings yield

Table 8.I The main ratios to be considered

 Crucial tip   Studying Table 8.I will help you to memorise the various ratios.

Limitations of ratio analysis

We can obtain more information about those firms (PLCs) that have to publish accounts.

- The **chairman's and directors' reports**, published with the final accounts, contain overviews of company performance.

- **Notes to the accounts** allow further analysis, e.g. a review of the age and type of assets.

- The **five-year summary** in the published accounts may contain statements of ratios.

Although ratios show trends and allow inter-firm comparisons, this is an insufficient guide to a firm's performance. One reason is that we know financial accounting information is **historic** in nature: it looks backwards at past performance rather than forwards. This means that, in effect, it is difficult to make accurate projections from the analysis.

Also, applying the **money measurement concept** (page 72) means that financial accounting deals exclusively with those items for which a monetary value can be given. This is again an incomplete analysis because it ignores issues such as the quality of the firm's workforce, any likely obsolescence of its products, and the strength of its market share and competition.

Finally, ratio analysis may also be **misleading**, e.g. where a firm 'window dresses' its final accounts.

Crucial concept   **'Window dressing'** occurs when there are attempts to boost a company's balance sheet position, often with regard to its (apparent) liquidity.

Examples of window dressing include:

- paying money into the firm's bank account, the amount being withdrawn shortly afterwards, in order to boost the year-end cash balance;
- with a group of companies, just before the year ends one company forwards a cheque to another with an overdraft, the cheque being used to pay off the overdraft – which would otherwise have to be shown in the group accounts – but the cheque is cancelled once this has been achieved.

SSAP 17 Accounting for Post Balance Sheet Events has helped control window dressing. Companies must reverse any transactions taken before the year end if these transactions were made to alter the appearance of their balance sheets.

 Crucial tip   Ratios may only give an approximate answer, e.g. if based on a one-off value taken from the balance sheet.

 Quick check
1. Name and describe **four** categories of accounting ratios.
2. Explain the limitations of ratio analysis.
3. What is 'window dressing'?

Section 2 — Profitability ratios

What are you studying?

In this Section, we introduce the first category of ratios, dealing with a firm's profitability. It is the role of these ratios to indicate how profitable the firm is by summarising the relationship between its profit, turnover and capital employed.

How will you be assessed on this?

You are typically given a set of final accounts. Questions based on profitability ratios test your ability to do two things: calculate the ratio accurately and comment on what the ratio indicates. To do this successfully, you must apply your general knowledge of how the ratio is calculated and what it seeks to show to the specific figures and scenario given in the question.

Here and elsewhere in ratio analysis, you may also be assessed on your understanding of the limitations of (profitability) ratios.

We already know that profitability measures a firm's **total profit compared to the resources used** in making that profit. As with other categories of ratios, the results of calculating profitability ratios allows **internal** analysis (trends in the firm's profitability) and **external** analysis (comparison with similar firms in the same industry) to take place.

Profit on its own is a relatively meaningless figure: it needs to be compared with turnover and with the resources used to create it.

Profitability ratios

1. RETURN ON CAPITAL EMPLOYED (ROCE)

'Simple':
$$\frac{\text{Net profit}}{\text{Capital employed*}} \times 100$$

'Detailed' (company)
$$\frac{\text{Profit on ordinary activities before interest and tax (PBIT)}}{\text{Capital employed*}} \times 100$$

(*Capital employed = Shareholders' funds + Long-term liabilities: i.e. total assets less current liabilities.)

ROCE shows the profitability of investment in the firm by calculating its percentage return.

This return can then be compared with expected returns from other investments. Companies tend to use the PBIT figure rather than profit after tax because the tax charge may vary from year to year (so using the profit after tax figure would not allow 'like with like' comparison). If we exclude debt (loan) capital, we would use the profit **after** interest figure.

The key rule is to compare like with like.

We can subdivide ROCE, the **primary** ratio, into two **secondary** ratios:

ROCE	=	**Profit margin**	×	**Asset turnover**
$\frac{\text{PBIT}}{\text{Capital employed}}$	=	$\frac{\text{PBIT}}{\text{Sales}}$	×	$\frac{\text{Sales}}{\text{Capital employed}}$

The **profit margin** ratio (see below) shows the level of the firm's profit margin on its sales; the **asset turnover** ratio (page 159) measures how efficiently the company's net assets are being used to generate its sales. **ROCE may therefore change as a result of either NP% and/or asset turnover changing.**

2. **NET PROFIT MARGIN (NP RATIO OR NP %) AND GROSS PROFIT MARGIN (GP RATIO OR GP %)**

$$\frac{\text{Net profit (PBIT)}}{\text{Turnover}} \times 100 \qquad \frac{\text{Gross profit}}{\text{Turnover}} \times 100$$

Crucial concept

The **NP** margin shows the percentage of turnover represented by net profit, i.e. how many pence out of every £ sold is net profit. The **GP margin** illustrates the percentage of turnover represented by gross profit.

Crucial tip

Since the NP% shows how many pence net profit per £ sales are being made, it indicates by how much selling prices can be cut (to cut the selling price = to cut the NP margin).

There is a close relationship between these margins: for example, any change in GP% should have the same 'knock-on' effect on the NP margin (if not, then the P&L expenses % will have changed). For example, check these summarised accounts of a firm:

	Year 1 (£000)	Year 2 (£000)
Turnover	100	200
Cost of sales	70	150
Gross profit	30	50
Expenses	20	20
Net profit	10	30

The year 1 £ figures also represent the **percentage** figures, i.e. the cost of sales is 70% of turnover (100%) and the GP margin is therefore 30%. The net profit margin is 10%, the difference being 20% expenses.

If we recalculate year 2 figures in percentage terms, we have 75% cost of sales and a 25% gross profit margin. Other things being equal, the NP% should be 5% (expenses last year were 20% of sales): it is, however, 15% because expenses have fallen to 10% of sales.

Quick check

1. Calculate the ROCE, GP% and NP% for Simon Travis (see Chapter 4, page 90).

2. Calculate the GP% and NP% of Gabriel Ltd (see Chapter 6, pages 129–30).

Section 3 — Liquidity ratios

What are you studying?

This Section shows you how to calculate the main liquidity ratios. These are used to assess the financial well-being of firms. As with Section 2, we explain not only how to calculate these ratios, but also what each of them tells us.

How will you be assessed on this?

As you know, you'll probably be given a set of final accounts on which the questions are based. Again, these questions test your ability to calculate the ratio accurately, and also to make appropriate comment on what the ratio shows. Assessment of liquidity ratios is often linked closely to the assessment of profitability and efficiency ratios.

Liquidity

Page 26 defined liquidity: fundamentally, it is **the amount of cash a firm can obtain quickly, in order to settle its immediate debts**. Although this firm may be able to survive in the short term without sufficient profit, it cannot survive for long without sufficient liquidity. In accounting, 'liquid funds' consist of:

- cash in hand and at bank;
- short-term investments and deposits;
- trade debtors.

These liquid funds must meet the demands made by trade creditors, tax payments to the government and the owners (e.g. shareholder dividends, or sole traders' and partners' drawings). The **cash** (or **operating**) cycle shown in Figure 8.1 summarises the way in which trading influences liquidity.

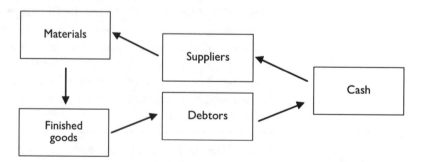

Figure 8.1 The cash cycle

The cash cycle is far more complicated in practice:

- the timing of cash flows will not coincide with sales and purchases/cost of sales – allowing and taking credit causes this difference;

- delays also occur with cash receipts, e.g. by increasing the credit period or through holding additional stock;
- taking credit will delay cash payments.

 Crucial tip   This is why firms need an efficient **credit control** system, to ensure constant cash flows into the firm.

Liquidity ratios

I. WORKING CAPITAL (CURRENT) RATIO

 Crucial concept   The **current ratio** is the ratio of current assets to current liabilities.

If current liabilities exceed current assets, the firm may have difficulty in meeting its debts. Extra short-term borrowing to pay off creditors costs the firm money (interest). If the firm sells assets to help meet its debts, it risks loss of production and future expansion. The standard 'textbook' ratios are 1.5 : 1 or 2 : 1, though in practice firms such as the major high-street retailers that have low debtor figures may have ratios in the region of 0.2 : 1 and still be 'safe'.

The key points are: (a) how does the firm's current ratio compare with those of its competitors? and (b) what trends are being shown?

Crucial tip   Don't confuse the working capital **ratio** with the working capital **figure** (i.e. the actual amount of working capital (net current assets)).

2. LIQUID RATIO ('ACID TEST' OR 'QUICK ASSETS')

Crucial concept   The **quick assets ratio** is the ratio of current assets minus stock to current liabilities.

This ratio tells us whether the firm can meet its short-term debts without having to sell any stock, which is regarded as the least liquid current asset. The prudence concept requires accountants to assume the firm will not automatically sell its stock, so stock is regarded as the least liquid current asset because it takes a long time to convert into cash.

As with the current ratio, a textbook figure for this ratio – often given as 0.8 : 1 or 1 : 1 – is meaningless without knowing both the nature of the industry and the trend as shown by a comparison with previous years.

 Crucial tip   We can also think of the 'debtor days', 'creditor days' and stockturn ratios (page 160) as types of liquidity ratio.

The next four liquidity ratios are more closely associated with the long-term solvency of the business.

3. DEBT RATIO

Debt ratios focus on **how much a firm owes in relation to its size**. This analysis indicates whether lenders are likely to loan additional funds given the level of the firm's debt.

 Crucial concept   The **debt ratio** is the ratio of total debts to total assets.

Here, a 50% figure is often regarded as the maximum. Again, the key consideration is the trend, i.e. whether this figure is rising or falling.

 Crucial tip   In calculating the debt ratio, we ignore long-term provisions and liabilities such as deferred taxation.

4. CAPITAL GEARING

Gearing analyses the different types of payments made to capital.

Crucial concept   **Gearing** calculates a company's prior charge capital as a percentage of its total capital. '**Prior charge**' capital carries the right to a fixed return (i.e. preference shares and debentures).

$$\frac{\text{Prior charge capital (long-term loans and preference shares)}}{\text{Total capital}}$$

Companies with more than 50% prior charge capital are called **high geared**; those with less than 50% are **low geared**. The level of gearing affects a company's ability to borrow fixed-return capital, especially if highly geared. In such a case a company may find it difficult to take out more loans. A highly geared company that has taken on these large loans may find that, if it can't meet the interest payments, the lenders force it to sell assets to recover their debts. Also, the more highly geared the company, the greater is the risk that shareholders won't receive a dividend distribution, and so it may be difficult to interest potential ordinary shareholders.

Crucial tip   We can examine the gearing position from different viewpoints: directors, investors (shareholders), and actual and potential lenders.

5. DEBT–EQUITY RATIO

Crucial concept   The **debt–equity ratio** is similar to the gearing calculation, comparing prior charge capital to ordinary share capital plus reserves.

$$\text{Debt-equity ratio} = \frac{\text{Prior charge capital}}{\text{Ordinary share capital} + \text{Reserves}}$$

Through focusing on the same area, we obtain similar information (a ratio of 100% or above here indicates high gearing).

6. INTEREST COVER

Crucial concept   The **interest cover ratio** shows by how much the profit before interest figure exceeds the interest charge.

$$\text{Interest cover} = \frac{\text{PBIT}}{\text{Interest charges}}$$

By calculating this, we can see how much the profit figure can fall before it is unable to meet the interest payments. A textbook ratio of 3 : 1 is sometimes suggested as adequate.

Quick check

1. For Edwood Ltd (see page 130), calculate these ratios:
   (a) current; (b) quick assets; (c) debt; (d) gearing; (e) debt–equity.

2. Calculate the interest cover ratio for Gabriel Ltd (see pages 129–130).

Section 4   Efficiency ratios

What are you studying?

In this Section you will study ratios that complement both profitability and liquidity ratios. The first – asset turnover – is closely linked to ROCE, and the three others, by focusing on current assets and current liabilities, are also indicators of liquidity.

How will you be assessed on this?

Once again you'll be given a set of figures and asked to calculate relevant ratios and make appropriate comments on the results. Since there are close links between these and other groups of ratios, questions test your knowledge of both efficiency and other ratios.

Firms need to **use their assets** as efficiently as possible. The efficiency of both fixed and current assets can be measured.

1. ASSET TURNOVER

$$\frac{\text{Sales}}{\text{Net assets}}$$

Crucial tip Remember you can use the capital employed figure if necessary, i.e. **Net assets = Capital employed**.

Crucial concept The **asset turnover ratio** is one of the 'secondary ratios' from ROCE (see above) and shows how efficient net assets have been at generating sales.

Asset turnover is therefore a measure of asset efficiency, i.e. how many £s worth of sales is generated by £1 worth of assets.

2. DEBTORS' COLLECTION PERIOD ('DEBTOR DAYS')

$$\frac{\text{Debtors}}{\text{Turnover}} \times 365$$

This liquidity (or efficiency) ratio shows the time, measured in average days, that it takes debtors to pay the firm. **Trend** is again the best guide, indicating the increasing or reducing efficiency of the firm's credit control system.

3. CREDITORS' COLLECTION PERIOD ('CREDITOR DAYS')

$$\frac{\text{Creditors}}{\text{Purchases}} \times 365$$

We can also calculate this 'liability' ratio in order to show the average length of credit (in days) the firm receives from its suppliers.

Crucial tip A rising figure for debtor days indicates a negative trend (customers are taking longer to pay), whereas a rising figure for creditor days is probably a positive sign (our credit period taken is increasing).

4. RATE OF STOCK TURNOVER ('STOCKTURN')

$$\frac{\text{Cost of sales}}{\text{Average stock}} \qquad \text{(stated as ' ... times per period')}$$

The purpose is to calculate how frequently the firm sells its stock. Stock must be valued at the **lower of cost or net realisable value** (another example of the prudence concept in operation).

Crucial tip An alternative way to calculate stockturn as 'stock days' is

$$\frac{\text{Average stock}}{\text{Cost of sales}} \times 365$$

Like debtor days and creditor days, the **trend** here is all-important. For example, a lower stockturn figure may point to slower trading and/or excessive stocks being held.

Crucial concept | The **debtor days**, **creditor days** and **stockturn ratios** can also make an important contribution when analysing a firm's liquidity position.

Quick check

1. Calculate these ratios for Simon Travis (see page 90):
   (a) debtor days; (b) creditor days; (c) stockturn.
2. Using your ROCE and net profit % calculations from the Quick check on page 155:
   (a) calculate Simon's asset turnover ratio;
   (b) show the relationship between the ROCE, NP% and asset turnover ratios.

Section 5   Investment ratios

What are you studying?

This final Section concentrates on those ratios that help actual and potential investors evaluate whether it's worthwhile investing in a company.

How will you be assessed on this?

It's the normal method, giving you information on the financial situation of a stock-exchange listed company, and asking you to calculate ratios and explain the results. With investment ratio questions you may well be given summary accounts for two companies, and asked to suggest which is the better investment. Since the value of a listed company is its market value, you will be given the share price as well as the information in the published accounts.

Actual and potential shareholders are interested in assessing the value of an investment in the (ordinary) shares of a company. They are particularly interested in two aspects of their investment :

- the **share price** (any increase here provides **capital** growth); and
- the **dividend** received, i.e. the **income** element.

1. **EARNINGS PER SHARE (EPS)**

$$\frac{\text{Profit available for ordinary shareholders}}{\text{Number of ordinary shares}}$$

Crucial concept | **EPS** shows the return on each ordinary share.

You've already studied how the EPS (for Merchant Magic – see page 129) can be calculated. If we assume Gabriel Ltd (page 129) has issued 200,000 £1 ordinary shares, we would use the 'profit on ordinary activities after tax' figure of £47,000 to calculate its EPS, i.e. 23.5p per share.

 Crucial tip — Remember FRS 3 (see page 121) requires 'earnings' (profits which can be paid out as ordinary dividend or retained) to be stated in the accounts.

2. DIVIDEND PER SHARE AND DIVIDEND COVER

Dividend per share will be stated by the company.

$$\text{Dividend cover} = \frac{\text{EPS}}{\text{Net dividend per ordinary share}}$$

Crucial concept — **Dividend cover** indicates the proportion of profit available for ordinary shareholders that has been distributed, and the proportion retained to fund future growth.

3. PRICE/EARNINGS (P/E) RATIO

P/E = Ratio of the current share price to the EPS

The higher the P/E ratio, the greater the confidence shareholders have in the company, and vice versa. (It's important to compare this ratio to those of other companies in the same industry.)

4. DIVIDEND YIELD

$$\text{Dividend yield} = \frac{\text{Share dividend for the year}}{\text{Current market value of the share}} \times 100$$

Crucial concept — The **dividend yield** indicates the actual return expected on the share by the shareholder.

 Crucial tip — We can use last year's dividend in the calculation.

5. EARNINGS YIELD

Dividend yield × Dividend cover = Earnings yield

Crucial concept — **Earnings yield** shows the EPS as a percentage of the current share price.

This ratio shows what the dividend yield would have been if all profits had been paid out as dividend.

We can see how some of these ratios are linked by studying this example. Here is summarised information for two companies:

	The Cartman Company £000	Kyle & Co £000
Profit on ordinary activities after tax	84	132
Preference dividend	5	10
Ordinary dividend	25	60
Retained profits	54	62
Ordinary shares issued:	1 million	2 million
Current share price	180p	160p

We can use these figures to calculate EPS, dividend cover, dividend yield and earnings yield.

- For The Cartman Company we have an EPS of £79,000/1,000,000 = 7.9p per share.

Crucial tip To get the ordinary shareholders' earnings, remember to deduct the preference dividend from the profit.

- We need the net dividend per ordinary share to calculate dividend cover: for The Cartman Company this is £25,000/1,000,000 = 2.5p per share. Dividend cover = 7.9/2.5 = 3.16 times.
- Dividend yield for The Cartman Company = 2.5p as a percentage of 180p market price = 1.39%.
- Earnings yield for this company = 3.16 x 1.39 = 4.39%.

Crucial tip We can check earnings yield by dividing 7.9 EPS by 180p price.

Quick check
1. State the method of calculation for the P/E ratio.
2. Explain the relationship between dividend cover, dividend yield and earnings yield.

Crucial examples

1. Sarah Osborne wants to invest some money in a company. Her friend has shares in a company called Carnival Ltd, and has lent Sarah the company's accounts.

Carnival Ltd
Summary profit & loss account for year ended 30 June 2001

	2001 £000	2000 £000
Turnover	2,833	2,645
Cost of sales	1,464	1,198
Gross profit	1,369	1,447
Expenses	812	912
Profit before interest and tax	557	535
Interest	125	75
Profit before tax	432	460
Tax	156	186
Profit after tax	276	274
Dividends	40	40
Retained profit	236	234

Carnival Ltd
Balance sheet as at 30 June 2001

	2001 £000	2001 £000	2000 £000	2000 £000
Fixed assets		5,061		3,503
Current assets:				
Stocks	500		455	
Debtors	520		345	
Bank	19		125	
	1,039		925	
Current liabilities:				
Trade creditors	608		342	
Proposed dividend	40		40	
Tax	156		186	
	804		568	
Net current assets		235		357
Long-term loan		(2,000)		(1,000)
Net assets		3,296		2,860
Capital and reserves:				
Share capital (£1 ordinary shares)		2,200		2,000
Profit and loss account		1,096		860
		3,296		2,860

Calculate appropriate ratios to help Sarah reach a decision on whether to invest in Carnival Ltd.

2. Using the figures for Kyle & Co. from page 163:
   (a) calculate EPS, dividend cover, dividend yield and earnings yield;
   (b) compare this company with The Cartman Company as a potential source of investment.

3. Define each of these ratio-related terms:

Asset turnover	Efficiency
Creditor days	Gearing
Current	GP margin
Debt	Interest cover
Debt–equity	Investment
Debtor days	NP margin
Dividend cover	Quick assets
Dividend yield	ROCE
Earnings yield	Stockturn
EPS	Window dressing

Answers

		2001			2000
1. **Profitability ratios:**		**%**			**%**
ROCE	276/3,296	8.4	274/2,860		9.6
GP %	1,369/2,833	48.3	1,447/2,645		54.7
NP %	276/2,833	9.7	274/2,645		10.4
Expenses %	48.3 – 9.7	38.6	54.7 – 10.4		44.3

(NB: The net profit figure used here is net of interest and tax; capital employed is taken as shareholders' interest, i.e. share capital plus reserves. We could use 'PBIT' and include the long-term loan as alternative bases.)

Analysis: ROCE has fallen owing to profits not keeping pace with additional capital invested. Sarah's investment would generate between 8 and 9 pence in the £ on present performance.

The NP% is broadly stable at about 10%, but the additional capital (and fixed assets) invested has not yet led to a major sales increase (though this will take time to achieve: there is a time lag between investment and increased turnover). There has been a fall in the GP margin: this could be as a result of cutting selling price to increase the volume of sales. The company has been efficient in reducing the expenses by nearly 6% when measured against turnover.

Asset turnover ratios are: 0.86 times (2,833/3,296) in 2001, and 0.92 times (2,645/2,860) in 2000. This allows us to review the primary and secondary ratios:

	ROCE		NP%	×	Asset turnover
(2001)	8.4%	=	9.7%	×	0.86
(2000)	9.6%	=	10.4%	×	0.92

The reduction in ROCE is attributable to the additional fixed assets (see balance sheet figures) not as yet being reflected in increased sales. In the future, any extra sales will increase asset turnover, which is likely to improve ROCE (though the net profit margin may fall, e.g. a major advertising campaign would increase the expenses % and reduce the NP margin).

Liquidity and efficiency ratios:		**2001**			**2000**
Current ratio	1,039/804	1.3 : 1	925/568		1.6 : 1
Quick assets	539/804	0.7 : 1	470/568		0.8 : 1
Debtor days	520 × 365/2,833	67 days	345 × 365/2,645	48 days	
Creditor days	608 x 365/1,464	151 days	342 × 365/1,198	104 days	
Stockturn (days)	500 x 365/1,464	125 days	455 × 365/1,198	139 days	
Gearing	2,000/5,296	38%	1,000/3,860		26%

Analysis: The current and quick asset ratios have fallen over the year, partly due to increased stocks and debtors. If this trend continues, the firm could find itself short of working capital. In addition, it is allowing its debtors to take an increasing credit period (from 48 to 67 days on average), but is itself benefiting from a very long credit period taken (up to 151 days). This may be a result of problems in paying creditors who, if they demand earlier payment, may cause problems for the company.

The company is not highly geared, though gearing has increased as a result of additional loans being taken out.

Investment ratios:		**2001**		**2000**	
Earnings per share	276/2,200	12.5p	274/1,800	15.2p	
Dividend per share	40/2,200	1.8p	40/1,800	2.2p	
Dividend cover	12.5/1.8	6.9 times	15.2/2.2	6.9 times	
Interest cover	557/125	4.5 times	535/75	7.1 times	

Analysis: Earnings and dividends per share have fallen in the year, due to additional capital being issued without a corresponding increase in profits after tax or in total dividend. There are substantial reserves as indicated by the high dividend cover, and the company could issue higher dividends in future though, with possible concerns over cash flow, this may not be possible.

Conclusion: There are some concerns over the company's falling liquidity position, as indicated by the ratios. It is also not highly profitable at present, though Sarah could monitor whether the additional investment in fixed assets increases sales and profitability in the next year or so.

2. (a) EPS: £122,000/2,000,000 = 6.1p per share.
        Dividend cover: ordinary dividend per share = £60,000/2,000,000 =
        3p per share; dividend cover = 6.1/3 = 2.03 times.
        Dividend yield: 3p as a percentage of market price 160p = 1.875%.
        Earnings yield: 2.03 × 1.875 = 3.81% (proof: 6.1 EPS divided by 160p
        price).

    (b)

	Cartman	Kyle
EPS	7.9p	6.1p
Dividend cover	3.16 times	2.03 times
Dividend yield	1.39%	1.875%
Earnings yield	4.39%	3.81%

Kyle's dividend yield is higher, but Cartman has the higher dividend cover,
greater EPS and better overall earnings yield. Of the two, Cartman
seems the better investment, but both have disappointingly low actual
returns – as measured by the dividend yield – when compared with
potential alternative investments (which may also be less risky).

3. Check your answers against the **Crucial concepts** in the Chapter.

Crucial reading and research

Reading

These books provide more information on ratio analysis:

Dyson, J. R. (1994) *Accounting for Non-Accounting Students*, 3rd edn. Pitman
    Publishing (ISBN 0 273 60435 X). See Chapter 8, 'Interpretation of
    accounts'.
Glautier, M. W. E. and Underdown, B. (1997) *Accounting Theory and Practice*,
    6th edn. Pitman Publishing (ISBN 0 273 62444 X). See Chapter 1, 'Inter-
    preting and comparing financial reports'.
Wood, F. and Sangster, A. (1999) *Business Accounting 1*, 8th edn. Financial
    Times/Pitman Publishing (ISBN 0 273 63742 8). See Chapter 33, 'Intro-
    duction to accounting ratios', and Chapter 48, 'An introduction to the
    analysis and interpretation of accounting statements'.

Research

You'll learn a lot more about the interpretation of financial statements by
continuing to read and study those published accounts we've already ad-
vised you to obtain. In these published accounts you'll find different policies and approaches regarding whether and how ratios are shown, and you
can also use them as sources from which to practise calculating ratios.

EXAMINATION
QUESTIONS AND ANSWERS

Here are some questions, to give you the chance to put what you've learnt into practice. We've included a marks guideline and also suggested a time limit.

Questions

Question I

The following accounts appear in the ledger of Neil Moore:

K. Sandwith			Dr	Cr	Balance
			£	£	£
April	I	Balance			75
	17	Purchases		225	300
	27	Bank	75		225

D. Williams			Dr	Cr	Balance
			£	£	£
April	I	Balance			500
	9	Bank		490	
		Discount		10	
	14	Sales	220		220
	21	Returns		40	180

(a) What is the relationship between Neil Moore and the people represented by these accounts? (2 marks)

(b) What document is associated with the transaction on the 14th? (1 mark)

(c) What was the rate of discount for the transaction on the 9th? (1 mark)

(d) What type of discount is this? (1 mark)

(e) Which entry above is associated with a credit note? (1 mark)

(f) How would the closing balances be shown in Neil Moore's final accounts? (2 marks)

(g) What benefit is there to Neil Moore by keeping accounts using this three-column approach? (2 marks)

Total: 10 marks

Suggested time: 10 minutes

Question 2

Neil Moore keeps a single account for rent and rates. As well as paying rent for one of his sites, he sublets another site. Here is his account for April.

Rent and rates

		£			£
30 April	Bank (rent)	4,800	I April	Balance b/d	1,100
	Bank (rates)	1,200	30 April	Bank (rent)	400
	Balance c/d	600		Profit and loss	5,100
		6,600			6,600

Neil gives you the following information:

● at the start of April he owed £1,200 for March rent, had prepaid rates £300, and had received £200 in advance from his tenant;

● at the end of April he owed £1,200 for April's rent, had prepaid rates £400 and was owed £200 by his tenant;

● in the month Neil had paid £4,800 for rent and £1,200 for rates.

Prepare separate accounts for:

(a) rent payable	(7 marks)
(b) rent receivable	(7 marks)
(c) rates	(6 marks)

showing all balances and transfers to profit and loss.

Total: 20 marks
Suggested time: 20 minutes

Question 3

Neil Moore's trial balance failed to agree and so he entered the difference in a suspense account. His draft profit and loss account showed a profit of £52,108, and the suspense account had a credit balance of £1,466.

Neil's accountant managed to locate these errors:

(i)   loan interest paid £100 had been posted to the loan account;

(ii) no entry had been made for the cost of power £426 used in the last month;

(iii) an invoice total of £164 was entered correctly in the sales day book, but was posted to the customer's account as £1,064;

(iv) one of the pages of this day book totalling £583 had not been posted to the sales account;

(v)   an entry in the purchases day book of £28 was not posted to the supplier's account;

(vi) the petty cash balance was incorrectly shown as £5 rather than £50.

(a) Record the entries required to correct the above in the journal.	(9 marks)
(b) Show the entries in the suspense account.	(7 marks)
(c) Calculate the effect of these errors on Neil's net profit.	(4 marks)

Total: 20 marks
Suggested time: 20 minutes

Question 4

During the night of 24 July, one of Neil Moore's buildings containing stock was damaged by fire, and some stock was destroyed. This stock was insured, but Neil has discovered that his stock records have also been destroyed. He has asked you to calculate the value of stock lost, and has supplied you with this information:

(i) Balances:

	I January £000	24 July £000
Stock (at cost price)	66	?
Trade debtors	19	23
Trade creditors	22	26

(ii) Transactions, January to 24 July:

	£000
Cash purchases	8
Cash sales	44
Receipts from debtors	157
Payments to creditors	137
Discounts allowed	5
Discounts received	4

(iii) Stock surviving the fire (at cost) £45,000.

(iv) Neil uses a 30% profit margin based on the selling price.

Calculate the cost of stock lost as a result of the fire.

Total: 25 marks
Suggested time: 30 minutes

Question 5

This is the trial balance for Chuck and Bob, who trade in partnership.

Trial balance as at 30 September 2001

		£	£
Capital accounts (I October 2000):	Chuck		30,000
	Bob		10,000
Current accounts (I October 2000):	Chuck		3,000
	Bob		5,000
Drawings for the year:	Chuck	7,000	
	Bob	9,000	
Purchases and sales		111,000	150,000
Stock, I October 2000		30,000	
Employee wages		14,500	
Selling and distribution costs		3,000	
Rent and rates		5,000	
Power costs		1,200	
Other expenses		5,300	
Cash at bank and in hand		4,500	
Debtors and creditors		14,000	11,500
Fixed assets		5,000	
		209,500	209,500

Additional information at 30 September:

(a) Stock at this date valued at £40,000.
(b) At this date, rent £1,000 was prepaid, and wages £500 accrued.
(c) Chuck had taken goods worth £1,000 for his own use, but no entry had been made in the books for this.

The partnership agreement states that the two partners share profits and losses equally. In addition:

• Chuck receives £12,000 and Bob £6,000 as salaries;

• each partner receives 5% interest on his capital account balance;

• Chuck is to be charged £200 and Bob £300 as interest on drawings.

Prepare:
(i) the partnership profit and loss account;   (20 marks)
(ii) the balance sheet;   (15 marks)
(iii) the partners' current accounts.   (15 marks)
                                          Total: 50 marks
                              Suggested time: 45 minutes

Question 6
These are the final accounts of Solomon Ltd for the year ended 31 March 2001. The company operates in an expanding market, and is in the process of improving its fixed assets.

Solomon Ltd: Profit and loss account for the year ended 31 March

	2001		2000	
	£000	£000	£000	£000
Turnover		4,500		3,000
Cost of sales:				
Opening stock	350		250	
Purchases	2,800		1,600	
Closing stock	(450)	2,700	(350)	1,500
Gross profit		1,800		1,500
Depreciation		200		150
Other expenses		600		550
Profit on sale of fixed asset		10		–
Operating profit		990		800
Interest paid		15		5
Profit before tax		975		795
Taxation		340		290
Profit after tax		635		505
Proposed dividends		200		100
Retained profit		435		405

Solomon Ltd: Balance sheet as at 31 March

	£000	2001 £000	£000	2000 £000
Fixed assets		1,135		640
Current assets:				
Stocks	450		350	
Debtors	360		250	
Bank	175		20	
	985		620	
Current liabilities:				
Creditors	180		90	
Dividends payable	200		100	
Taxation	340		290	
	720		480	
Net current assets		265		140
Total assets less current liabilities		1,400		780
Long-term liabilities:				
Loan		(125)		(50)
		1,275		730
Capital and reserves:				
Called-up share capital (£1 ordinary)		600		500
Share premium account		60		50
Profit and loss account		615		180
		1,275		730

In August 2000, a fixed asset originally costing £45,000 with depreciation of £18,000 was sold.

(a) Prepare a reconciliation between cash flows from operating activities and operating profit for the year ending 31 March 2001. (15 marks)

(b) Prepare a cash flow statement for the year ending 31 March 2001. (25 marks)

Total: 40 marks

Suggested time: 30 minutes

Question 7

These ratios have been calculated from a set of accounts.

Gross profit margin	40%
Net profit margin	15%
Selling expenses/sales	5%
Stock turnover	6 times per annum
Working capital ratio	1.2 : 1
Quick assets ratio	0.6 : 1
Debtor days	24
Net profit to total assets	10%
Bank balance £8,400	25% of current assets

Additional information:

(a) The calculations are based on a 300 working day year.

(b) All sales are made on credit.

(c) There were no drawings during the year.

(d) There are no long-term liabilities.

(e) Profit and loss expenses are grouped under two headings:
    Selling expenses
    Administrative expenses.

Construct the final accounts in as much detail as possible.

Total: 35 marks

Suggested time: 40 minutes

Answers

Answer I

(a) K. Sandwith is Neil Moore's creditor (account contains 'purchases', i.e. purchases from Sandwith); D. Williams is his debtor (account shows sales to Williams).

(b) Sales invoice, sent by Neil Moore to Williams.

(c) 2% (£10 as % of £500).

(d) Cash discount (also known as settlement discount).

(e) 21st: Neil Moore sends Willliams the credit note, indicating that Williams's account has been credited with the value of the goods returned.

(f) Sandwith, £225 in the total creditors (balance sheet current liabilities): Williams, £180 in the total debtors (balance sheet, current assets).

(g) The running total (balance) can be seen at a glance.

Answer 2

Rent payable

April 30	Bank	4,800	April 1	Balance b/d	1,200
April 30	Balance c/d	1,200	**April 30**	**Profit and loss**	**4,800**
		6,000			6,000
			May 1	Balance b/d	1,200

Cr balance: rent owed **by** Neil Moore
(current liability)

Rates

April 1	Balance b/d	300	**April 30**	**Profit and loss**	**1,100**
April 30	Bank	1,200	April 30	Balance b/d	400
		1,500			1,500
May 1	Balance b/d	400			

Dr balance: rates prepaid (current asset)

Rent receivable

April 30	**Profit and loss**	**800**	April 1	Balance b/d	200
			April 30	Bank	400
			April 30	Balance c/d	200
		800			800
May 1	Balance b/d	200			

Dr balance: rent owing **to** Neil Moore
(a current asset)

Answer 3

(a)   **Journal**

(i)   Loan interest   100
         Loan   100
(ii) Power   426
         Accruals   426
(iii) Suspense   900
         Debtor   900
(iv) Suspense   583
         Sales   583
(v)   Suspense   28
         Creditor   28
(vi) Petty cash   45
         Suspense   45

(b)   **Suspense account**

Debtor	900	Balance	1,466
Sales	583	Petty cash	45
Creditor	28		
	1,511		1,511

(c) Net profit   52,108
     Less loan interest   (100)
     Less power   (426)
     Add sales   583
     Corrected net profit   **52,165**

Answer 4
Stock bought (£):
Cash purchases 8 + Paid to creditors 137 + Discount received 4 = 149 value of purchases for which cash paid/discount.

Add closing creditors (stock bought but not yet paid for), less opening creditors (in the cash paid figure, but for last period's stock) = 149 − 22 + 26 = **153 stock received in the period**.

Stock sold (£):
Cash sales 44 + Cash from debtors 157 + Discount allowed 5 = 206 cash received.

Add closing debtors (stock sold for which no cash received this period), less opening debtors (cash received this period relating to last period's stock sold) = 206 − 19 + 23 = 210.

Calculate stock at cost price (to compare with stock at cost price bought): 210 × 70% (30% margin = 70% cost price) = **147 stock sold at cost price in the period**.

Actual stock should be:
Opening stock 66 + Stock received 153 − Stock sold 147 = **70**
Stock left after fire = 45
Stock lost in fire = 70 − 45 = 25

Answer 5

Chuck and Bob: Profit and loss account
for year ended 30 September 2001

	£	£
Sales		150,000
Less cost of sales:		
Opening stock	30,000	
Purchases (– 1,000 drawings)	110,000	
Closing stock	(40,000)	100,000
Gross profit		50,000
Less expenses:		
Wages + 500 accrued	15, 000	
Selling expenses	3,000	
Rent and rates less 1,000 prepaid	4,000	
Power	1,200	
Other expenses	5,300	28,500
Net profit		21,500
Interest on drawings: Chuck		200
Bob		300
		22,000

		£	
Salaries:	Chuck	12,000	
	Bob	6,000	
Interest on capitals:	Chuck	1,500	
	Bob	500	20,000
Residue of profit			2,000
Share: Chuck (½)		1,000	
Bob (½)		1,000	(2,000)

Chuck and Bob: Balance sheet as at 30 September 2001

		£	£
Fixed assets			5,000
Current assets:	Stocks	40,000	
	Debtors	14,000	
	Prepaid expenses	1,000	
	Bank	4,500	
		59,500	
Current liabilities:	Creditors	11,500	
	Accrued expenses	500	
		12,000	
Net current assets			47,500
Net assets			52,500
			£
Capitals:	Chuck		30,000
	Bob		10,000
			40,000
Current accounts:	Chuck	9,300	
	Bob	3,200	12,500
			52,500

Current accounts

	Chuck	Bob		Chuck	Bob
	£	£		£	£
Drawings	8,000	9,000	Balances b/d	3,000	5,000
Interest on drawings	200	300	Salaries	12,000	6,000
Balances c/d	9,300	3,200	Interest on capitals	1,500	500
			Residue of profits	1,000	1,000
	17,500	12,500		17,500	12,500
			Balances b/d	9,300	3,200

Answer 6

(All figures £000.)

Overall cash increase £175 − £20 = £155

(a)   **Solomon Ltd:**

Reconciliation between cash flows from operating activities and operating profit for the year ending 31 March 2001:

	£
Operating profit	990
Depreciation (2001 figure used)	200
Profit from sale of fixed assets	(10)
Increase in stocks (450 − 350)	(100)
Increase in debtors (360 − 250)	(110)
Increase in creditors (180 − 90)	90
Net cash inflow from operating activities	**1,060**

(b)   **Solomon Ltd:**

Cash flow statement for year ending 31 March 2001

		£
Net cash inflow from operating activities		1,060
Returns on investment and servicing of finance:		
Interest paid (2001 P&L figure)		(15)
Taxation (2000 figure, paid in 2001)		(290)
Capital expenditure (see workings below)		
Cash from sale of tangible fixed assets	37	
Purchase of tangible fixed assets	(722)	(685)
Equity dividends paid (2000 figure, paid in 2001)		(100)
Financing:		
Share capital issued (+ 10 share premium)	110	
Loan capital issued (125 − 50)	75	185
Increase in cash		**155**

Workings for capital expenditure   £

Cash from sale:	Cost of fixed asset	45	
	Depreciation	(27)	
	Net book value	18	
	Add profit on sale	10	
		38	cash received from the sale
		£	
Purchases:	Closing value (net)	1,135	
	Add back depreciation	200	
		1,335	
	Opening value (net)	640	
	Less net value of asset sold	(27)	
		613	

Difference 1,335 − 613 = 722 purchased

Answer 7

1. Bank £8,400 = 25% of current assets, so total current assets = £8,400 × 4 = £33,600.
2. Current assets to current liabilities = 1.2 : 1, so since £33,600 = 1.2, current liabilities total £33,600 / 1.2 = £28,000.
3. Quick assets = 0.6 : 1, so bank and debtors = 0.6 × £28,000 = £16,800: since bank = £8,400, debtors are £16,800 − £8,400 = £8,400.
4. Total current assets = £33,600, less bank and debtors £16,800, so closing stock = £16,800.
5. Debtor days (debtors × 300/sales) = 24: debtors are £8,400, so £8,400 × 300/sales = 24: sales = £2,520,000/24 = £105,000.
6. Gross profit = 40% of £105,000 = £42,000: cost of sales = £63,000.
7. Net profit = 15% of £105,000 = £15,750: total expenses = £42,000 − £15,750 = £26,250.
8. Selling expenses = 5% of £105,000 = £5,250 so admin expenses = £26,250 − £5,250 = £21,000.
9. Stockturn = £63,000/average stock = 6: average stock = £10,500: since closing stock is £16,800, opening stock must be £4,200.
10. Opening stock £4,200 + purchases − closing stock £16,800 = cost of sales £63,000: purchases = £75,600.
11. Net profit £15,750 = 10% of total assets: total assets = £157,500: fixed assets = £157,500 − £33,600 current assets = £123,900.
12. Opening capital + net profit £15,750 = net assets £129,500 (fixed assets + working capital), so opening capital = £113,750.

Trading, profit and loss account

	£	£
Sales		105,000
Less cost of sales:		
Opening stock	4,200	
Purchases	75,600	
Closing stock	(16,800)	63,000
Gross profit		42,000
Administrative expenses	21,000	
Selling expenses	5,250	26,250
Net profit		15,750

Balance sheet

	£	£
Fixed assets		123,900
Current assets:		
Stock	16,800	
Debtors	8,400	
Bank	8,400	
	33,600	
Current liabilities	28,000	5,600
		129,500
Opening capital		113,750
Net profit		15,750
		129,500

INDEX

Learning Resources
Centre